THE
CREATIVE
SHOPKEEPER
•••

THE CREATIVE SHOPKEEPER

...

LUCY JOHNSTON

Thames & Hudson

CONTENTS

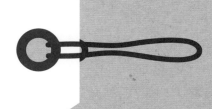

INTRODUCTION

...

'*Excite the mind, and the hand
will reach for the pocket.*'
- Harry Selfridge, 1909

A NEW AGE OF ENTREPRENEURIAL RETAILING

In this world of commercial excess and endless options, where everyday essentials can be purchased with complete convenience and limited mindful engagement, a clear movement is evolving through which global audiences seek more meaning in their chosen shopping experiences.

The purchase of objects that we value beyond pure necessity, that we seek for their desirability, their inspirational nature and the ways in which they can improve our lives, becomes an activity imbued with a higher purpose. The whole experience - the act of searching for that perfect gift; the narrative into which we buy; the knowledge and expertise imparted to us along the way; the visual messages and sensory stimulation that we absorb; and the service we receive - takes on the role of an event. Through this experience we collectively seek a greater level of stimulation for the mind, cultural understanding and a memorable story with a lasting impression.

Certainly, in today's highly commercialized landscape, online retail leads the field in terms of audience volume, logistical efficiency, competitive price and the ability to offer a 'long tail' range of products. However, the efficient transaction and fulfilment of an order are not always the pinnacle of what consumers seek, and

e-commerce is certainly not the nemesis of real-world retail that it has so often been predicted to be. It has simply sparked a change in the rules of engagement, to the benefit of us all.

Faced with a mass of competition, real-world retail experiences must innovate in order to define their competitive difference, and this is being embraced wholeheartedly. Compelling new retail propositions are emerging in our shopping streets and destinations, proving a welcome antidote to a noisy, over-saturated, intangible and often fickle digital world. Appetite, support and appreciation are also growing constantly, most notably on the independent retail scene. Where these enterprises cannot compete with e-commerce in terms of volume, scale and price, they more than make up for it through quality, expertise, service and community engagement - four key factors that determine the joy of experience that has long attracted and retained customers.

In a digitally influenced society where savvy audiences with ever-shorter attention spans are proficient at editing out irrelevant information and commercial noise, these retailers' stories and offerings must work exceptionally hard to be refreshing and different, authentic and considered, to cut through the often raucous competition and to gain and retain the attention of an audience. Additionally, when the majority of our daily interaction with commercial and cultural content is increasingly led by quickly digested imagery rather than words, real-world retail environments must acknowledge and respond by striving to both offer a refined service experience and be captivating to the eye. Only thus will they be captivating to the wallet as well.

THE NEW RULES OF ENGAGEMENT

We are experiencing the growth of an independent retail scene of a standard that is unprecedentedly high. A healthy rebellion is transforming our streets, and gathering momentum; the traditional retail establishment is waning, and a flexible, independent diversity is rising. This is a time of nimble, efficient business models and smart shopkeepers who are drawing on the retailing traditions of previous decades but also benefiting from the fast-paced technological innovations of the present decade to build robust, adaptable brands that bring renewed energy to our shopping destinations.

This entrepreneurial movement is being fuelled by a range of factors: the results of advances in culture and technology, combined with a changing economic climate. It is encouraged and facilitated by customers' maturing awareness of authentic values; by jaded city workers looking for satisfying new outlets for their time and talent; and by an improving attitude to property leasing, allowing shorter and therefore more affordable leases to be approved. Great opportunities are opening up for shopkeepers of all styles to bring their distinctive stories and products to market, to find appreciative audiences and to give the business of retail their best shot.

For these businesses, investing smartly in physical retail space - whether temporary or longer-term - can prove a stronger and more cost-effective strategy than traditional advertising or marketing spend. Nothing beats getting a product into the hands of potential customers, and involving them in the brand, for a tangible and longer-lasting impact.

To be discovered and coveted in today's hectic retail scene requires not only passion, a great product and great presentation, but also a clear strategy and well-planned execution across many channels of communication. So, although the narrative focus of such entrepreneurial businesses might be on the physical retail proposition, and many might benefit from strong word of mouth, these shopkeepers are not shunning the online marketplace. Rather, they are embracing it, learning from it, balancing it and using it to support their shop experience and service as a whole.

The entrepreneurial shopkeeper understands and embraces the opportunity to create a multifaceted retail proposition.

While the shop provides visual enticement, the necessary sensory encounters and the personal service, digital platforms are the engine that casts a wider net. So, in many cases, these dynamic retail concepts are supported by online retail platforms - and certainly by website and media platforms - ensuring a wider reach and benefit through building recognition, connections and sales.

This necessarily multilayered approach, and the complex considerations of today's retail landscape and of consumer expectations in general, is a challenge that demands that the concept of creative retailing play an ever more central role in commercial differentiation. The notion of a creative approach to both commerce and communication is proving increasingly powerful in setting the stage for retailers to differentiate themselves and thrive.

SETTING THE STAGE FOR MAGIC

Writing in 1925, the retail pioneer Gaston-Louis Vuitton spoke of requiring 'the skills of a stage director' when creating his iconic brand's visual displays. This is more the case for today's pioneering retailers than it has ever been before. Like the stage of a theatre, shops offer a platform upon which to share with audiences a wide range of stories and ideas, and take them on a journey of discovery. However, unlike a conventional stage, a shop invites that audience to step through the theatrical 'fourth wall' and become immersed in the particular viewpoint that is on offer. Harry Selfridge, another

true retail entrepreneur, was one of the first to understand and capitalize on this concept, from a promotional perspective. He revolutionized the retail experience in the early twentieth century, transforming shopping into a form of entertainment.

We often hear references to 'retail theatre', and this concept is certainly crucial to creating competitive, memorable shopping experiences, if the term itself is now ubiquitous and losing its meaning. Beyond creating a visual spectacle, the theatre of the modern retail environment requires an exceptionally intricate mix of attributes: careful consideration of communication, acute attention to every detail and the ability to remain flexible and responsive to new ideas and demands. In theatrical terms, modern retailing should take cues as much from the 'improv' genre as from the fully staged production.

ENTER THE CREATIVE SHOPKEEPER

Faced with this most complex of marketplaces, the modern shopkeeper must demonstrate creative ingenuity and the bold, imaginative use of modest budgets. Today a more diverse and challenging set of skills and resources is needed than has ever been required before.

With only a small team, the modern shopkeeper must not only think and act creatively in terms of brand positioning, presentation and strategy, but also - in most cases - wear the hats of business owner, designer and producer of the product on offer, and manager of the shop, logistics, e-commerce, digital content and marketing. They must have a truly entrepreneurial approach that allows them to be constantly open to change and new influences, curating and steering their business to respond to cultural shifts and stay relevant in a fast-paced industry.

These demands make the creators of the success stories featured in this book particularly notable for their dedication, passion and creative endeavour. Beyond beautiful, cool or charming, these shops are physical stories of ingenuity, resourcefulness and entrepreneurial spirit. They represent the vision of pioneering individuals with a shared belief: that modern retail might be complex and challenging, but it also holds the potential for the magic that offers the treasured moments of joy that society is constantly seeking.

A COMPENDIUM OF CREATIVITY

This book celebrates the spirit, determination and inventiveness of some of the most inspired independent shopkeepers and retail entrepreneurs around the globe today. It also forms a compendium of ideas and suggestions for simple techniques and cost-effective solutions from which to draw inspiration when setting up shop, whether temporary or permanent, and for both first-time and seasoned traders.

Each of the ten chapters introduces a key area of consideration in order to create a retail experience with impact, explored through a careful selection of case studies and supported by expert insight from the international shopkeepers featured, as well as from designers and other industry figures.

It is worth noting that, while each case study demonstrates an approach to the theme of its chapter, and explains the relevant techniques in practice, they are also exceptional examples of retail in a more rounded sense. So do take the time to study and appreciate each one in detail.

As proven by the businesses in this book, and a great many more besides, the independent retail community is thriving, challenging and delighting us in the most competitive of markets and creating something new every day. I hope that you find plenty in this compendium of creativity to inspire you to do the same. Nowhere is the creative potential of commerce in all its forms being more imaginatively and effectively demonstrated than in the resurgent communities of independent shops and entrepreneurial retail businesses that are drawing, and will continue to draw, appreciative audiences worldwide.

PROPS & ICONS

...

CREATE MEMORABLE FIRST ENCOUNTERS BY
INTRODUCING PROPS AND POINTS OF VISUAL
INTERACTION THAT CAPTURE THE CHARACTER
AND STYLE OF YOUR BRAND.

...

*'In a busy marketplace, not standing
out is the same as being invisible.'*
- Seth Godin, 2003

Although it is certainly true that 'a good product sells itself', in a busy marketplace the quality of one product over another may not be apparent to the glancing customer. So, even with a strong product, there is still a skill to be honed in understanding how to stand out from the crowd, how to communicate succinctly and how to cut through the noise and competition to draw an audience and get that product into a prospective customer's hands. As the writer and entrepreneur Seth Godin so convincingly says, a business has limited value if it doesn't find its own way to stand out. Once it is noticed by the customer - if the product is as good as anticipated - the selling process will probably follow naturally, and the repeat visits and word-of-mouth benefits will flow.

Market research tells us that a commercial business has literally just a few seconds to grab the attention of a prospective customer, and captivate them into further investigation. So, for all retailers regardless of their product, the focus must in substantial part be on creating a visual message and call to action that are as strong and as compelling as possible.

This process revolves around carefully considered 'moments' of visual interaction, and physical interaction if possible or appropriate, to gain competitive advantage. This can take the form of full-scale scene-setting, or it can revolve around simpler touches and techniques. The approach doesn't necessarily require a big budget, but a focused understanding of what makes the business stand out, clarity of purpose and authenticity of voice are essential. This enables the shopkeeper to conceive ingenious ways of communicating an appealing narrative, thus helping audiences to understand and remember the product.

One such simple yet effective way of quickly communicating that differentiating narrative is through the introduction of visual icons and props, which can act as engaging and emotive anchors in a frenetic market. Such devices must be introduced carefully, so as not to create a distraction; they must have a clear reason for being; and they must help, rather than hinder, the transmission of a clear, memorable message. These icons can be an effective way to summarize a complex concept, to explain the intangible benefits and differentiating attributes of a product, and to conjure a specific emotion or sensation in the prospective buyer.

Desirable feelings include nostalgia, delight, amusement, excitement, aspiration and freedom. Where they must be generated at speed, in the moment of glancing, the required message is often most concisely and effectively conveyed through visual statements or physical actions, rather than descriptive written copy. For the most part, in a noisy commercial environment and after the initial glance or moment of interaction, a visual or active image lasts longer in the mind, and as a differentiator in the memory,

than words. It is not always the case, but the notion that 'images speak louder than words' certainly holds true when it comes to selling a concept, and drawing an interested audience, in an already 'loud' landscape.

The visual devices used as part of this approach may be the products themselves, presented playfully, if - in their form, tactility, style or presentation - they have enough presence to jump out and speak. More often it is the scene with which the product interacts that creates the necessary memorable context - the use of a separate iconic device, structural feature or series of props that defines and benefits the business proposition or product concept in order to communicate that all-important, powerful supporting narrative.

The technique of introducing smart, eye-catching visual statements can have a strong storytelling power in any scenario. It is particularly effective, however, for temporary and transient shop concepts, such as pop-up shops, sampling activities or kiosk-style propositions, which do not have a traditional, contained shop space of their own. In these scenarios, props and icons focus attention and create a halo effect, a 'zone' within which the story unfolds. This visually defined place into which the customer can be welcomed and drawn gives the impression of a contained space, even without walls.

Whether it is a display fixture or a graphic device, a lighting feature or a characterful heritage object, if presented carefully and meaningfully - not placed purely for the sake of it - a contextual symbol can build a richer story, helping to capture the attention, imagination and understanding of the customer. Poetic and theatrical, playful and expressive, energizing and inspirational, such symbols can embody the summary of an attitude, a viewpoint or a lifestyle statement, silently demonstrating a dedication to exceptional retail craft. They also speak volumes of the

care and attention given by a shopkeeper to
the overall experience of their business,
of their clarity of purpose, and of the
value and respect they give to the product
itself. They characterize the pride and
pleasure the shopkeeper takes in the little
touches, in identifying the significant
details that they understand will increase
the customer's conscious or unconscious
perception of value, and in finding those
unique elements that will have the most
positive effect on the audience they want
to impress.

   Above all, the effective use of props and
icons is about understanding how the product
proposition, and the surrounding narrative,
will be most beneficially perceived by the
onlooker. If done well, this will encourage
those first moments of visual interaction
to become moments of physical interaction
and then purchase.

THE FLOWER STALL
TOKYO, JAPAN
...

The artistic intention behind this eye-catching mobile flower shop is that it appears only during new moons. It pops up on street corners, in parks and in stations around Tokyo, unannounced and unseen until the day it reveals itself in each location.

It is the brainchild of the well-known Japanese flower artist and botanical sculptor Azuma Makoto, who founded the JARDINS des FLEURS flower shop and workshop in Tokyo. He originally worked as a trader in the Ota Market, one of Japan's largest flower and produce markets, from which he continues to draw inspiration. His wide-ranging floral designs and artistic installations around the world, and his work for the shows and events of many of the world's leading luxury fashion houses, are celebrated.

An original pop-up concept, this structure is intended as both a creative installation and a promotional prop to showcase Makoto's imaginative work and his commercial floral decoration business. The stall itself is not commercial as such - the florist simply hands out a single flower as a gesture of happiness to each person who passes by - but the format and execution are commercially applicable.

The stall, a modified warehouse cart, has a mechanical steam-punk aesthetic and incorporates a water tank as well as a small heated greenhouse, which emits a gentle glow of light and steam and within which new buds are presented and grown. Despite its unusual styling, the scale is similar to that of traditional market stalls, so it rolls neatly in among the range of market and pavement offerings across the city.

'One does not know where this mobile flower shop will appear today. We prepare flowers from the local area, and when all are given away, the stall closes. This is not for commercial purposes, but solely as a kind of social project. I call this flower stall "Kibou", meaning "Hope".'
- Azuma Makoto

Address
Various locations, Tokyo, Japan
Designer
Azuma Makoto (www.azumamakoto.com)

Constructed on the scale of a
traditional market stall, this
custom installation makes an
eye-catching alternative.

TIPS

. . . .

TIP 1 - Create a memorable moment in the city with an unexpected take on a retail tradition. Give your audience a photo opportunity and encourage them to share.

. . . .

TIP 2 - Whether it is big or small, careful and thoughtful execution of your pop-up ensures that the visual impression reflects your dedicated attitude to your business and the quality of the products you have to offer.

PRESS LONDON
LONDON, UK
...

The first of a new breed of British cold-pressed juice companies, PRESS, was founded by Georgie Reames and Ed Foy and began life with just two juicers, a bathtub and some ice.

The entrepreneurial Brits, who launched London's first cold-pressed juice bar and kickstarted a juice revolution, were inspired by the fresh juice culture of the United States. Both had lived and worked there, and they wanted to bring the taste and health benefits of raw and unpasteurized juices to appreciative, health-conscious audiences in the United Kingdom.

After perfecting their first juice recipes, Reames and Foy initially set up a simple stall in London's Old Street station to get their first bottles into the hands of busy City workers. Thinking creatively about their presentation, in order to stand out and give their new brand an engaging personality, they settled on a vintage bathtub full of ice. This eye-catching set-up won them much attention, as did the quality of their juices. In fact, the initial batch sold out on the very first morning, prompting them to work through the following nights to keep up with demand.

The brand evolved quickly from there, winning a fast-growing following of keen customers. From further market stalls and sampling events, they have since developed a chain of permanent shops around the capital, and the now iconic and covetable bathtub is still very much in evidence as a central feature of their merchandizing scheme. It also appears in miniature, as a table-top display, at their many events and tastings.

'When we were thinking about our display, we recalled how in the United States they display anything on ice. It looks so inviting. So we devised the idea of a vintage bathtub filled with ice, to give a British twist. I bought one on Gumtree and painted it in my garage!'
- Ed Foy

Address
Various locations, London, UK
Website
www.press-london.com
Founders
Georgie Reames and Ed Foy

NO PASTEURIZATION
(NO UHT OR HPP)

PRESSED
NOT
BLENDED

TIPS
. . . .

TIP 1 - Stand out from the crowd
and build recognition by thinking
creatively about your presentation,
remembering the importance of
attention to detail for maximum
impact.

. . . .

TIP 2 - By all means experiment
with display solutions and props
that are surprising and capture the
imagination, but ensure that they
retain a relevant purpose in the
context of what you are selling.

PR≡SS

PEDDLER'S CREAMERY
LOS ANGELES, USA
...

After working in an ice-cream shop while he was at secondary school, Edward Belden had a vision of opening his own ice-cream business - but with a difference. Peddler's uses only organic ingredients, highlights local produce and incorporates sustainability into all aspects of its operation. It strives for its customers to leave with a delicious ice cream, a smile on their face and the knowledge that they are buying from a company that promises to leave a smaller footprint on the Earth.

The shop itself is fitted out with reclaimed materials and incorporates the vibrant and joyful colours of the ice creams, while the focus is on a whimsical, interactive kinetic installation in the centre of the shop floor. This static bicycle, with attached cog-and-chain mechanism, enables customers and employees alike to pedal away on the spot, powering the churn that mixes the ice-cream base of cream, milk, sugar and egg yolks as it freezes, to make sure the ice crystals are kept small.

Customers can simply buy an ice cream at the counter, but many volunteer to contribute to this sustainable practice by donating their time and energy to pedal in exchange for a free scoop. One batch takes 20-25 minutes to make using this method, and the Peddler's Creamery team take it in turns to pedal, keeping fit at the same time. As well as the ice cream that is churned during opening hours, they produce a few batches of ice cream each night, ready for the following day's trade.

'I wanted to create a unique way of serving delicious ice cream, while doing it in a sustainable way. The best moments are when I hear customers say that it's the best ice cream they have ever had, and then discovering that we make it using the bicycle!'
- Edward Belden

Address
458 South Main Street, Los Angeles, CA 90013, USA
Website
www.peddlerscreamery.com
Founder
Edward Belden
Store Designers
Oonagh Ryan (www.oonaghryan.com)
and Joe Alguire (www.jaws.ac)

Raw textures and playful colours create a friendly feel, encouraging visitors to get involved in the craft process.

Flavors

COFFEE
VANILLA
SNICKERDOODLE
CARROT CAKE
PEANUT BUTTER
ORANGE CHOCOLATE
SALTED CARAMEL

TIPS

......

TIP 1 - Actions not words. If your product involves a specific production process, consider putting that on show and letting the live action tell the story.

......

TIP 2 - If your process can be presented in an accessible format, explore how you could encourage your customers to get involved in a hands-on way that benefits everyone.

......

TIP 3 - Involving your customers will naturally generate word of mouth, so ensure that it is positive by considering their contribution and how you reward that involvement.

Visitors pedal their way towards earning a free scoop by helping to churn a traditional pail of ice cream.

WILDE EYEWEAR
BARCELONA, SPAIN
...

Having been a collector of vintage sunglasses for more than two decades, Wilde's founder, Cao Azuaje, opened his first shop - now one of four outlets - as an experimental space in which to develop and present his own iconic collectible eyewear pieces, which are handmade in Barcelona. He also offers vintage pieces and other favoured designs that he and his team source from around the world.

The shop environment, created with design partner Robert Adalierd, is a tribute to the expressive urban style and spirit of 1980s music and experimental music culture in general - a passion of Azuaje's and an ongoing inspiration for his product designs. The flagship shop features Azuaje's large collection of original boom boxes as display surfaces and props, stacked around the space to set a distinctive, moody scene that is far removed from the bright, clinical style of so many contemporary eyewear stores.

The immersive music culture theme is enhanced with low-level, club-style lighting. Display walls are lined with details and fixtures - including acoustic foam panels, audio wiring, mixing-desk equipment and LEDs - that further give the customer the impression of being cocooned in a club or recording studio.

In this landscape of props and non-traditional display surfaces, the individual sunglasses are placed casually. As if laid down by a passing musician, they are ready to be discovered by the steady stream of treasure-hunting musicians, music fans and style aficionados from around the world, who frequent the stores and take great pleasure in buying into the brand's characterful culture and strong statements.

'We started to produce our own furniture, and are constantly redecorating the shops ourselves. It is important to create the sensation of experimentation and space for self-expression, just like in our business. We use our shop as a kind of art curation, always looking for something unique and personal.'
- Robert Adalierd

Address
Calle Avinyo 21, Barrio Gótico, Barcelona 08002, Spain
Website
www.wildesunglasses.com
Founder
Cao Azuaje
Store Designers
Cao Azuaje and Robert Adalierd (www.adalierd.com)

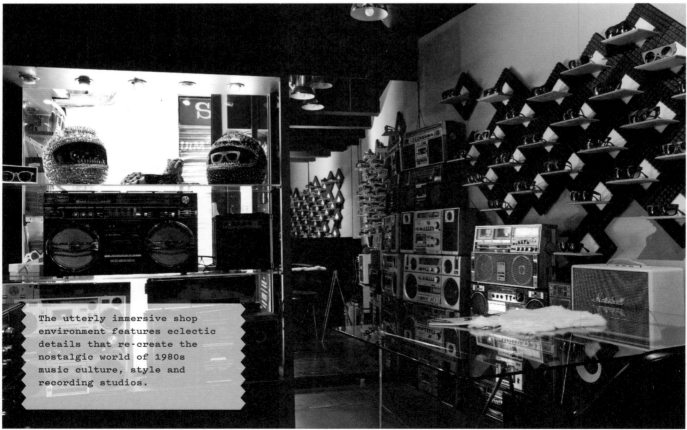

The utterly immersive shop
environment features eclectic
details that re-create the
nostalgic world of 1980s
music culture, style and
recording studios.

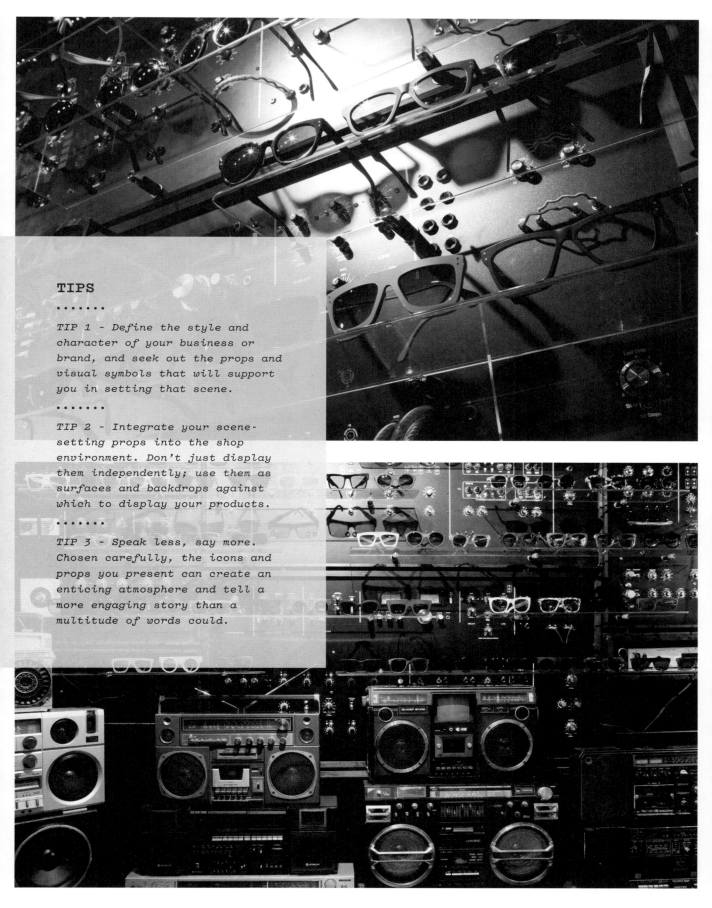

TIPS

. . . .

TIP 1 - Define the style and character of your business or brand, and seek out the props and visual symbols that will support you in setting that scene.

. . . .

TIP 2 - Integrate your scene-setting props into the shop environment. Don't just display them independently; use them as surfaces and backdrops against which to display your products.

. . . .

TIP 3 - Speak less, say more. Chosen carefully, the icons and props you present can create an enticing atmosphere and tell a more engaging story than a multitude of words could.

STORY
NEW YORK CITY, USA
...

The founder of the curated retail concept STORY, Rachel Shechtman, approaches her shop as an ever-changing magazine, choosing a theme or trend for each 'issue' and taking a carefully edited viewpoint, the narrative of which runs across both the selection of merchandise and the fit-out of the space. She trades in the style of a gallery, presenting each theme for between three and eight weeks, and the shop closes for a week or so in between to allow a complete re-imagination of the space before reopening to unveil the next story.

The one constant across these iterations of the shop's look and feel is the technique of using the STORY logo as a creative icon to introduce each narrative theme. Variations have included Wellness Story, Love Story, Colour Story, His Story and Disrupt Story. This visual device is displayed centre-stage in the shop, and frames the title of each new story in brackets that form the 'O' of the logo, creating a concise and effective backdrop for the topical scene that unfolds across the shop.

For every 'issue' of STORY the shop environment is rebuilt completely, a process that involves collaborating with a host of creative and commercial partners. Experience is at the centre of the business strategy: there is a very busy events programme, and the shop employs 'storytellers' rather than sales staff. Savvy when it comes to the power and influence of visual communication, STORY's team is active on Instagram and creates original content for the website every day.

'We opened the shop with this idea of being a platform to try new things, and explore different themes that interest us and that we feel are relevant to our diverse audience. Like a magazine, we think about how we can create a compelling story - both visually and through the content we present.'
- Rachel Shechtman

Address
144 10th Avenue, New York, NY 10011, USA
Website
www.thisisstory.com
Founder
Rachel Shechtman
Logo Designer
Stefan Sagmeister (www.sagmeisterwalsh.com)

Each new 'story' involves a total refit of the shop. This one included a garage door, complete with graffiti.

TIPS

. . . .

TIP 1 - Consider how your
brand identity can become a
smart, dynamic device to help
you tell an evolving story,
keeping your concept fresh,
energetic and enticing.

. . . .

TIP 2 - Images speak louder than
words. Experiment with defining
your business through carefully
chosen icons, single words and
strong visual props.

. . . .

TIP 3 - Coordinate the narrative of
your story from the windows right
through to the back of the shop.
Think about the details that help
to create the complete journey.

The logo is styled for each
story and featured clearly,
from the windows through to
the feature wall in-store.

Realizing that their target audience did not necessarily think of visiting them on the busy high street and paid little notice to traditional advertising, the team at menswear label Brothers decided to get out on the road and visit them instead - with the aim of presenting smart, functional clothing for the urban traveller.

A highly crafted contribution to the booming pop-up movement that is constantly evolving in cities across the world, the resulting Suitcase Store is proof that by thinking and behaving more like smaller, nimble independents and getting creative and flexible with new ways to market, larger brands can make a positive impact on saturated consumers who are looking for authenticity and a good story. In order to keep up with a target audience that is often on the move, the Suitcase Store was sent on a tour of the country's largest airports and railway stations - always keeping to the strong narrative of travel and high quality on the go - with great long-lasting effect.

This pop-up activation focused on promoting quality through craftsmanship, as demonstrated in every detail of the build and execution. The presentation of every item has been carefully thought through to ensure that each product has its own dedicated nook, hanger or shelf.

The unexpected appearance of this oversized suitcase - complete with built-in speakers to set the right mood, and a complimentary shoe-shining service - certainly surprised and delighted passing customers. Transactions were managed seamlessly with the revolutionary wireless payment platform iZettle, which has changed the game for independent retailers that have no fixed address.

'What conveys the travel theme better than if the store itself is simply a suitcase, ready to be packed and on the move to the next stop? So we built Brothers Suitcase Store - a huge suitcase that held a great little shop.'
- Arvid Axland, creative lead

Address
Various locations, Sweden
Agency
Pool (www.pool.se)
Designers
Philip Arvidsson and P.J. Lindqvist
Build
Attributverket (www.attributverket.se)

BROTHERS

SUITCASE STORE

BROTHERS.SE/SUITCASESTORE

TIPS

· · · · · · ·

TIP 1 - Oversized props can
be very effective, if presented
with attention to detail and
in a way that ensures a relevant
and beneficial relationship
with the product.

· · · · · · ·

TIP 2 - It's a good exercise to
imagine how you could condense your
proposition into a portable format
with impact. This will give clarity
to your offering on any scale.

NAVIGATION & CHOICE
...

ENSURE FEELINGS OF DELIGHT AT PURCHASES
MADE, THROUGH CLEAR PRESENTATION OF
THE CHOICES, HELPFUL EXPLANATIONS
AND THOUGHTFUL SUGGESTIONS.
...

'Nowadays there is such a great variety
of goods to buy that shops have also to
be a source of information.'
- J.M. Richards, 1938

Choice has long been a compelling factor
in attracting an audience, encouraging
them to dwell and inspiring them to return
for future transactions and to explore
further. The perception of choice is linked
to feelings of excitement, optimism and
potential, and empowers the customer to
control their decisions.

While the purchase of daily necessities
demands simplicity, and most people prefer
to have fewer options to choose from in that
context, the mindset can be very different
for an audience that chooses shopping as an
event, a source of pleasure or a cultural
experience. During these alternative forms
of engagement, a wealth of product options
can represent an enticing opportunity with
delightful potential, and exploring them
can be a welcome journey of inspiration
and discovery. However, if this desirable
consumer behaviour is to be encouraged and
repeated, the final purchase and the general
outcome of the experience must result in
satisfaction, rather than confusion.

Whether the offering is tightly curated or broadly spread, in this world of constant 'information overload' the shopkeeper must help the customer to navigate the products in a way that inspires and excites them, yet also explains and reduces complication. The art is in good communication and presentation, so that the options do not become daunting and the resulting journey remains a pleasure.

Navigation, interaction with a product range and the process of choosing encompass everything from introducing and explaining the product, offering comparisons and giving thoughtful reasons for the various physical and visual ways in which the customer is steered through the space, the experience of the transaction and the way they are served. Good navigation tactics allow a product range to be explored in a way that focuses the eye and concentrates the mind, rendering the decision-making process clear while retaining the pleasurable feeling of anticipation inherent in having a wealth of desirable options. Such a process will end for the customer with satisfaction over time well spent, confidence in the outcome and pleasure in engaging with the shopkeeper.

This approach requires careful editing and presentation - what we might refer to as 'curation' - regardless of the volume of options. The original notion of curation related to the act of organizing and maintaining a collection of artworks or artefacts. The same is true of good navigation and presentation in a shop. Now a well-used - even over-used, and frequently misunderstood - term throughout the retail industry, curation in this context must entail clear comparisons between objects or offerings, defining and explaining each one individually while tying the whole collection into one narrative.

We live in a high-speed modern culture that is increasingly powered by quickly digested visual communications, and most of us have notably fewer text-based encounters.

In this environment, the most effective techniques for helping customers to navigate naturally revolve around visual and image-led cues and triggers, whether using physical imagery or techniques that conjure certain images or sensations in the mind's eye.

This means that considered design and creative expression are vital, as are the unexpected, delightful and clever solutions for presenting many options that define one shop proposition from another. Customers are more likely to engage with and take longer to explore a proposition if they are shaken out of the habitual 'daze' of the modern audience - the subconscious result of being faced with a crowded marketplace - by thoughtful expressions and new ways of seeing. Such ways of seeing must challenge the norm, impart genuinely surprising, useful and informative content, and create a desirable context for new encounters.

In a busy, noisy commercial environment, it takes a high level of creative artistry to give a customer that all-important sense of excitement on viewing the bigger picture - the curated ideal - but then steer them carefully through the process of choosing and purchasing in a way that leaves them truly satisfied that they have made the best decision. In such a scenario, of course, the customer is more likely to return, so it is also the most satisfying outcome for the retailer. After all, the concept of creative shopkeeping is not just about pleasing the customer, but also about making this path a joyful, fulfilling experience for the shopkeeper.

In crafting a mutually satisfying scenario, it benefits both the customer's journey and the shopkeeper's experience if the customer is involved in and encouraged to interact with the process, rather than remaining passive so that the shopkeeper makes all the effort. The traditional adage 'Tell me and I forget, teach me and I remember, involve me and I learn', as imparted by the great luminary Benjamin

Franklin, very often holds true in retail. When we learn, we are prone to develop a considered viewpoint that we will then act on.

Customers are more likely to engage with the products and follow through to purchase when they are involved physically in the exploration and discovery of a new solution or treasured object. Through this conscious engagement, and by leading the customer through a methodical process of understanding, their anticipation is enhanced and their confidence and conviction that they are making the right choice increases greatly.

Searching for premises where their workshop, office and shop could be combined, the brothers and business partners Kamiel and Martijn Blom found and renovated an old industrial garage. By returning the building to its original atmosphere, they have created a space that perfectly suits the concept of their growing business: seeking out and restoring beautiful industrial lights salvaged from the abandoned factories of former East Germany, and crafting new pieces from found industrial artefacts.

The lamps, which are displayed across plain walls and surfaces, have great visual impact as a collection. But within these displays, much care is taken to give each lamp the individual celebration it deserves. Presented on the wall alongside each piece is a photo of the place where it was found and an explanation of the process of 'revaluing' it - the story of its rediscovery.

Expanding on this sharing of knowledge, the buyer of each piece also receives a 'passport', a small booklet that documents the origins of the object, including photos and descriptions of the unique design features and distinctive DDR aesthetic. The brothers initiated the passport because they felt it was important to raise cultural awareness and to communicate that these objects are also part of a historical legacy. The passports have had the unforeseen positive side effect of becoming an authentic promotional tool in the homes of the customers.

Those customers want to experience and understand the process of making, so another important feature of the space is the transparent wall between the workshop and the shop, offering glimpses into the place 'where the magic happens'. The space's wide glass frontage allows the full story to be told from the street, too.

'By styling the space in line with our brand principles, we created a place where people can really experience our work. Our products are given the attention they deserve. People not only see the value of the objects, but can also catch a little bit of the adventures we get into in finding these treasures.'
- Kamiel Blom

Address
Chrysantenstraat 20, 1031HT
Amsterdam, The Netherlands
Website
www.blomandblom.com
Founders
Kamiel and Martijn Blom

To celebrate each lamp design,
a plaque explains the process
of finding and 'revaluing' it.

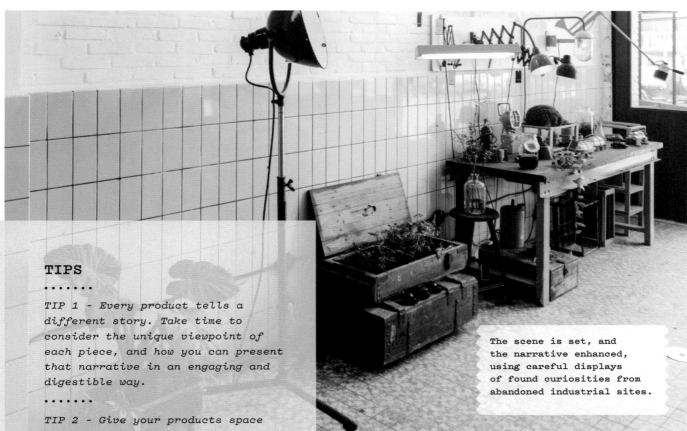

TIPS
· · · · · · ·

TIP 1 - Every product tells a different story. Take time to consider the unique viewpoint of each piece, and how you can present that narrative in an engaging and digestible way.

· · · · · · ·

TIP 2 - Give your products space to breathe and be appreciated individually. An insightful, gallery-style approach to displaying your offering will increase the emotive value of each piece.

· · · · · · ·

TIP 3 - Imagine how your product will speak once it is taken home. Think about the details that accompany it, to give your customers the confidence that they made the right choice.

The scene is set, and the narrative enhanced, using careful displays of found curiosities from abandoned industrial sites.

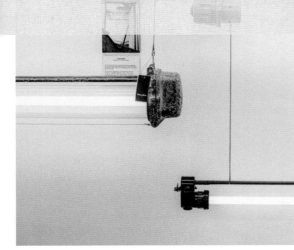

The founders of this unusual bookshop aim to inspire a fresh appreciation of the printed word and the way book-lovers can browse and discover new titles. The idea is to move away from the constant noise and artificial 'you might also like' culture of online shopping and embrace once more the possibility of chance encounters with great works that one might never otherwise find.

To encourage serendipitous discovery, the books are organized by theme rather than in traditional categories. The imaginative topics include 'Sea and sky', 'Enchantment for the disenchanted' and 'Mothers, madonnas and whores'. However, when required, the staff can also search the digital catalogue to enable a visitor to navigate directly to a specific title on the shelf. The shop's curatorial team is assisted by guest experts from across the publishing industry - including international authors - who are invited to curate their own shelf spaces with favourite titles and recommended reads.

The undulating cocoon of shelving, which lines the side walls from floor to ceiling, is inspired by the fantasy short story *The Library of Babel* (1941) by the Argentinian writer and librarian Jorge Luis Borges. This irregular formation creates natural segments, partitions and nooks where visitors can tuck themselves to read a new-found treasure. The flowing horizontal lines are punctuated by a varied collection of reading lamps, attached directly to the shelves, while the mirrored back wall and ceiling give the compact shop a feeling of greater spaciousness and enhance the sense of unbounded potential in the range of reading matter.

'The formation of the shelves allows themes and groupings to be layered, so a book of poetry might be displayed right above one on evolutionary psychology, expanding the opportunities for joyful chance encounters.'
- Sam Aldenton

Address
65 Hanbury Street, London E1 5JP, UK
Website
www.libreria.io
Founders
Rohan Silva and Sam Aldenton
Designer
SelgasCano (www.selgascano.net)

Books are organized non-traditionally by theme to encourage serendipitous discovery and to capture the imagination.

TIPS

. . . .

TIP 1 - Explore imaginative
and surprising ways of ordering
your displays, and inspire your
customers to think differently.
Don't do what everyone else
does without considering why.

. . . .

TIP 2 - Helping customers
to navigate the choices doesn't
necessarily mean editing down
the options. A wealth of choice
can be appealing, but facilitate
navigation with clear explanations
and direction.

. . . .

TIP 3 - Give your customers the
space to make their choices, and
invite them to take their time
appreciating the various options.
Relaxed browsing leads to more
satisfying purchases.

Flowing horizontal lines of books
are punctuated by an eclectic
collection of reading lamps,
attached directly to the shelves.

GERMINA
MEXICO CITY, MEXICO
...

This health-food shop, which sells a wide variety of dried produce in bulk, reinterprets the essence of Mexico's traditional market stalls in a permanent space that retains a relaxed relationship between shopkeeper and customer. From the product labelling around the space to the basic, hand-finished, customizable packaging, the simple, practical language of the shop emphasizes the rituals of the produce-focused market experience, bringing to the fore the name, weight and price of each product.

In this compact footprint, rather than restricting the airiness of the space by adding a store room, the bulk dry goods are stored in a striking central feature - a wall of simple, clearly labelled wooden boxes in a scaffolding framework that references a market stall. Customers can clearly view and navigate the range of options, and might even be reminded of items they had forgotten, supported by advice from the staff.

The tradition of the weighing scale is at the core of this service-led experience, and is part of the branding. The shopkeeper's vintage unit is placed at the centre of the main display wall, enhancing the ritual and pleasure of serving. The displays involve rustic wooden boxes, reusable hessian sacks, and wooden boards for the counter-top samples. A brown-paper pad on the wall is used to display handwritten daily specials. The seeds, grains and cereals are weighed and prepared for each customer, and presented in recycled brown-paper cones, bags and airtight glass jars.

'The storage system is a modern take on the traditional market stall, making the practical aspect a strong part of the aesthetic proposal, visible throughout the shop and from outside. It adds to the personalized shopping experience, where everything is packaged specially for each customer.'
- Orlando Fernández, designer

Address
Querétaro 225 Roma Norte,
Cuauhtémoc, 06700 Mexico City, Mexico
Designer
Savvy (www.savvy-studio.net)

Clearly labelled storage boxes become the central display feature, and also help visitors to navigate the range on offer.

Cacahuate

Semilla de Amapola *(Poppy Seed)*

Cacao *Orgánico*

Garbanzo *Orgánico*

Piñón *Blanco y Rosa*

Mijo

Avena *Orgánica*

Trigo

Alubia

Avellana

Linaza *Orgánica*

Lenteja *Verde y Roja Orgánica*

Ajonjolí *Orgánico*

Semilla de Calabaza

Macadamia *Orgánica*

Chía *Orgánica*

Amaranto *Orgánico*

Quinoa *Perlada, Roja y Negra*

Semilla de Girasol

Almendra *Orgánica*

Nuez *Orgánica*

Semillas, Arroces Granos, Nueces, Legumbres, Cereales, Frutos Secos

The vintage scale takes centre stage, giving a nod to a time when personal service was more common.

GERMINA

L-20 GRANOS Y SEMILLAS

Teff

Espelta
Orgánica

Pistache

Corazón
de Hemp
Orgánico

Kamut
Orgánico

Trigo
Sarraceno
(Buckwheat)

Arroz
Sushi

Farro
Orgánico

Centeno
Orgánico

Arroz
Salvaje

Arroz
Blanco de
Morelos

Basamati

Arroz
Jazmín

Arroz
Integral
Orgánico

Arroz
Arborio y
Carnaroli

GERMINA

The shop service is over
the counter only, ensuring
a personal, insightful and
satisfactory experience for

Customers can bring their own containers and attach a sticker, or choose from a range of packaging options.

TIPS
. . . .

TIP 1 - Clearly labelled products, with concise explanations, allow your customers to take their time making an initial judgement of the options.

. . . .

TIP 2 - Explore creative ways of presenting additional stock that will add to the visual appeal of your shop and help customers understand the available options.

. . . .

TIP 3 - Consider adding a personal touch to your service by packaging each customer's order on the spot. Simply wrapping with care can enhance the feeling of having made a good purchase.

A simple brown-paper pad displays daily specials, and doubles as wrapping material for purchases.

HAND-EYE SUPPLY
PORTLAND, USA
...

Hand-Eye Supply specializes in workwear, tools and materials for creative professionals. It is the brainchild of the co-founders of Core77, an independent publishing company whose mission is to serve the needs and interests of working designers. The shop is intended to extend that mission by bringing together the various pieces of the 'creative life'.

Matching the attention to detail inherent in the working practices of the shop's customers, the design of the space demonstrates an exceptionally high attention to detail in the selection of products, in the visual merchandizing and in the design of the fixtures and furnishings themselves. The structural design plays on the concept of the wireframe, a familiar prototyping device that is employed in the creative process, and that gradually fills in as solid ideas take on form. The system was custom-fabricated, and is deliberately tactile and functional. It is designed to display prominently the methods and materials of its construction, all of which will be familiar to the audience.

The space is bright and orderly and the products clearly arranged, with a sense of enjoyment and promoting an ethos of DIY, self-education and methodical exploration. The well-stocked modular units offer a range of ways to browse, inspired by different creative environments, ensuring that the experience is sensory, joyful and playful.

The venue also serves as the West Coast office for Core77's editorial staff, and hosts the company's events and working projects. The flexible structural segments and fixtures allow it to be reconfigured in response to changing use, and areas can be partitioned off when necessary.

'The descriptions in our online store focus on the history and interesting aspects of the products. These serve as education notes for the staff and give them a starting point for personal conversations. Additionally, each product gets a hand-typed tag, sometimes with a fact or two.'
- Laurence Sarrazin

Address
427 NW Broadway, Portland, OR 97209, USA
Website
www.handeyesupply.com
Founders
Laurence Sarrazin, Eric Ludlum, Allan Chochinov and Stuart Constantine

TIPS

. . . .

*TIP 1 - If you stock a variety
of different types of product,
get creative with how you display
each one, to give texture and
interest across the whole shop.*

. . . .

*TIP 2 - Look to other sectors
for new ideas for displaying
your products. Your customers
will appreciate the inspiration
and the fresh take on how to
navigate the product offering.*

Feature portraits integrated into the display walls picture the shop's real customers in their own creative studio environments.

The design of the modular walls enables a range of open display and closed storage units to be swapped in and out as required.

A variety of irreverent display styles celebrate each product individually, elevating the pleasing patterns of simple objects.

PALOMINO BLACKWING PENCILS

When the much-admired grandfather of Pedro, João, Ricardo and Tiago Cortiço died, the four brothers inherited his business of sourcing and selling rare and replacement Portuguese ceramic tiles. It came with an enormous collection of tiles that he had been buying as discontinued lines since 1979, as the Portuguese tile industry went through decline and gradual closure. The quartet felt a responsibility to their country's industrial heritage, so they wanted to continue the family business. They have evolved it into a more contemporary proposition, opening a new city-centre space that is part library, part museum and part shop.

The Cortiços now hold more than 900 different patterns in their vast commercial collection, and are asked daily for help with finding matches and specific designs. For this reason, being able to visualize the collection and efficiently find a particular design are crucial to the service they offer.

The deep, space-saving shelving solution in the centre of the store allows a great many tile designs to be displayed at any time, and doubles as effective and safe storage for the heavy, fragile boxes. The dazzling patchwork effect changes daily as the tiles are sold and boxes replaced, standing out beautifully against the neutral grey tones of the rest of the shop.

In the middle of the shop, a large table presents four wooden boxes that showcase tiles in similar fashion to a vinyl record shop, encouraging browsing and a tactile experience. Behind this is a functional counter, custom-made by the brothers, and beyond that is a workshop, in which they develop new products and engaging packaging solutions that present the tiles as fashionable treasures.

'We have some 900 patterns in our collection, and still we keep sourcing more. So the way we store and display them is very important to a clear vision. We are also developing a database, but for now the best way we know is to display them as we do.'
- Ricardo Cortiço

Address
Calçada de Santo André 66,
1100-497 Lisbon, Portugal
Website
www.corticoenetos.com
Founders
Pedro, João, Ricardo and Tiago Cortiço

With so many individual
designs, visual navigation
is critical, so a display
grid has been introduced
on surrounding surfaces.

TIPS
·······

TIP 1 - Sometimes, when every single product is different, the only way to explain the choice is to display as many as possible. But do stick to a clear methodology and structure.

·······

TIP 2 - The eye can process a variety of image-based options quicker than it can written ones, so, where there are complex options, keep your displays and explanations visually engaging.

·······

TIP 3 - Choices are often emotional as much as they are rational, so allow your customers to get tactile and explore the products with their hands.

To encourage hands-on browsing, many of the tiles are displayed in boxes, in the style of vinyl records.

This award-winning Argentinian bicycle brand is on a mission to encourage the community to adopt the bicycle as a sustainable mode of urban transport. Founded by the industrial designer Natan Burta, the company promotes the local manufacture of products that have a long life and require little maintenance, using high-quality components and craftsmanship.

The company began by refurbishing old bike frames, and manufacturing its own handlebars, leather saddles and baskets to give them a new identity. The popularity of the venture has meant that it has evolved fast, and Monochrome now develops its own designs as well.

The simple shop was developed sustainably and on a modest budget, with the remit that it should be flexible and easy to install. The bikes themselves provide the colour and structural interest, against a simple, neutral space of wooden crates and white-painted surfaces that form seats and exhibition platforms in the centre. A long panel of wooden pigeonholes along the side wall displays bike parts and accessories, while special metal hooks were designed to suspend the various styles of wheel rim from the ceiling.

At the back is the workshop, where bikes are assembled and fixed; it is painted a vibrant yellow to create a focal point for visitors and to make the maintenance of the bikes into a central activity. To one side of the entrance, a low table and a wall panel - presenting all the individual bike parts as an exploded three-dimensional diagram - defines the area where customers can devise and assemble their own custom-made model.

'Our mission was to create an environment to convey our sustainable design mission. Everything is carefully presented so that customers can clearly understand the process and all the options. We love that the workshop is in full view so you can see every customer as they are specifying their own bike.'
- Natan Burta

Address
Gorriti 5656, Palermo, Buenos Aires, Argentina
Website
www.monochromebikes.com
Founders
Natan Burta and Luciana Panczuch
Logo Designer
Estudio Nidolab (www.nidolab.com.ar)

The bike-building process is divided into clear sections, as the customer moves down through the long space.

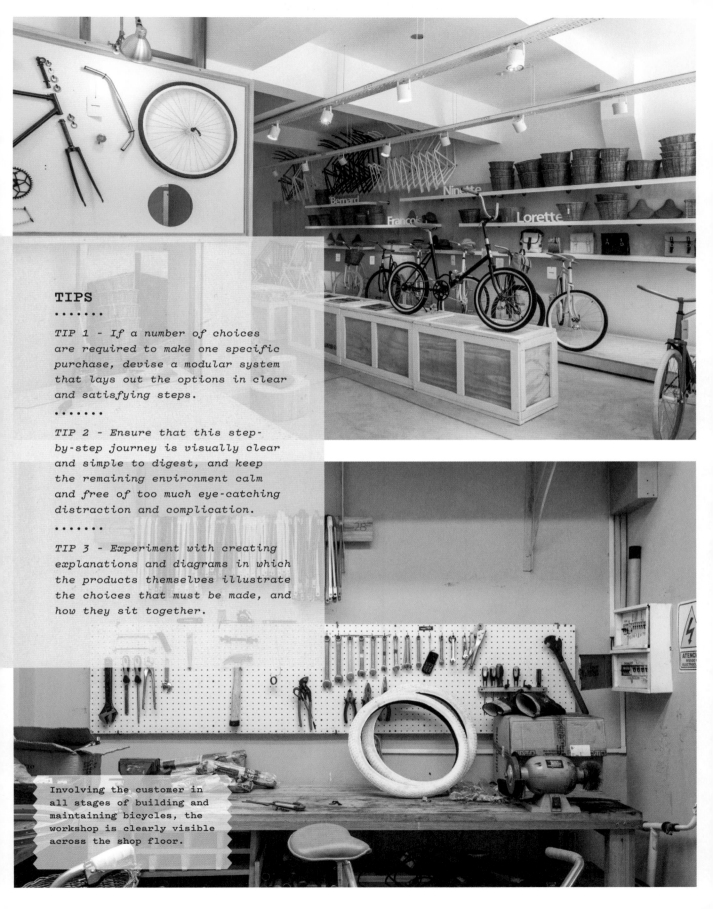

TIPS
· · · · · · ·

TIP 1 - If a number of choices
are required to make one specific
purchase, devise a modular system
that lays out the options in clear
and satisfying steps.
· · · · · · ·

TIP 2 - Ensure that this step-
by-step journey is visually clear
and simple to digest, and keep
the remaining environment calm
and free of too much eye-catching
distraction and complication.
· · · · · · ·

TIP 3 - Experiment with creating
explanations and diagrams in which
the products themselves illustrate
the choices that must be made, and
how they sit together.

Involving the customer in
all stages of building and
maintaining bicycles, the
workshop is clearly visible
across the shop floor.

JOURNEY & DISCOVERY
...

ENCOURAGE EXPLORATION AND MOMENTS
OF DISCOVERY BY CREATING AN INVOLVING
JOURNEY THAT PLACES THE PRODUCTS
WITHIN A NARRATIVE CONTEXT.
...

'Buying is a profound pleasure.'
- Simone de Beauvoir, 1949

In our advanced commercial landscape, customers making everyday purchases are required less and less to make an effort. Services are increasingly honed to cater to every whim, reducing challenges or obstacles and speeding the recipient through every step of the process, from seeking and finding to narrowing down the options to transaction and delivery.

Alongside the unquestionable benefits of this scenario - which include saving us from frustration and stress, and giving us back our precious time to be spent on more rewarding activities - are some very real, if subconscious, side effects that are not so positive. Perhaps most notable among these is the lack of the satisfaction that would come from having made the effort to achieve the result. Where we might previously have felt that the plethora of daily tasks is a burden, we now feel unsettled, aware of the ever more apparent disconnect between effort and receipt, achievement or personal involvement.

At a basic level, humans need challenge and purpose in order to thrive. We have an inherent drive to seek out new ideas, to head for new horizons and to find meaning in what we are doing. In the modern world, the pace of change, and the lack of requirement for day-to-day effort, has the second drawback of shortening our attention span. We therefore actively look for stimulation to give us fresh inspiration and a way of constantly feeding our appetite for satisfaction through attainment.

A third perceived side effect could be understood positively: our frustration at the lack of meaning we get from a task that has required little effort. Our advanced lifestyles and the notion of 'modern conscious' - making time to listen to our conscience - make us hanker for greater meaning in our actions. As the daily act of purchasing becomes easier and ever more efficient, we increasingly want to demonstrate that we have made the effort and taken the time to make considered, positive gestures towards those around us. We are therefore increasingly attempting to spend time on the actions that we feel are most worthwhile, and that benefit not just us but also others. It is a way of obtaining satisfaction from a different angle.

In reality, in this busy world in which people constantly want a unique story, experience or stimulant, shopping is a natural attraction. Everyday, monotonous aspects aside, the act of shopping quite simply gives us pleasure and purpose, as the French feminist writer Simone de Beauvoir recognized in the clarity of her thought on the subject. We realize that the journey itself, and all that we tackle, explore and achieve along the way, offers us our fix of fulfilment.

Ultimately, as de Beauvoir acknowledged, it is the act of purchasing that gives us the moments of joy and satisfaction we crave. If we automate that activity we destroy the meaning and therefore the opportunity for a satisfying outcome.

This explains the recent rise of the narrative retail environment, a concept and style of retailing in which the customer is taken on a welcome journey of surprise, delight and discovery.

The act of seeking, finding and buying sparks in the customer the feelings of satisfaction and attainment that they find lacking elsewhere. The narrative retail experience is a source of desirable inspiration, new information and thought-provoking encounters. In providing the appeal of the new, the different, the unusual, this style of retailing greatly satisfies a modern 'hunter-gatherer' mentality.

Creating such environments successfully is an art in itself, and requires a truly creative approach to shopkeeping. Much is intuitive, and little of it can be taught as such; the skill is in crafting a rich and authentic experience that the customer will take their time to explore before stumbling on their personal holy grail:

the 'found treasure' that represents the time, consideration and (most notably) effort that they have put into such a personal discovery. Whether that is a purchase for themselves or for someone else, such a journey-led experience enables a story to be woven around the transaction, ticking those boxes of satisfaction, differentiation and proof of endeavour.

Such narrative concepts are often sizeable endeavours that offer plenty of reasons to dwell for prolonged periods of time, with space to journey physically through the proposition until curiosity is sated and the hunter-gatherer satisfied. However, the effect of a compelling journey can be achieved on a smaller scale, too; just think of the appeal of the age-old flea-market stall piled high with potential treasure. The key is in the careful and considered explanation of the proposition: pointing out the unique aspects and the one-off offers, hinting at the here-today-gone-tomorrow limited-edition finds, and

playing to the feeling of anticipation
that somewhere within the space lies
the perfect found treasure, with all
its associated meaning.

Above all, this style of retailing
involves strong visual curation, with
either full scene-setting or smaller,
thoughtful encounters. The context must
be wider and deeper than a simple collected
retail offering in itself. It is about
making connections and telling stories,
and, above all - as the visionary Harry
Selfridge understood so well - inspiring
the mind as much as the eye, in order to
inspire the heart to purchase.

A.G. HENDY & CO
HASTINGS, UK
...

Having worked as a photographer, a writer, a chef and a stylist for magazines for more than twenty years, Alastair Hendy wanted to bring his expert eye for curation to his own retail project. The result, his much-admired homewares shop, began as a place for him to share and sell the collections of useful things he had sought out over the years. It has evolved from there, with an ever-widening collection of well-sourced products, and more recently also introducing a cosy kitchen restaurant.

Hendy sources and curates his beautiful offering with a focus on functional beauty: practical goods that are made to last, and suited to both the modern and the traditional home. The products are simple, sound, honest and enduring, and throughout the warren of rooms and across floors, the adventurous visitor can discover a wealth of treasures ranging from enamelware to brooms, felt slippers to antique glass, and washtubs to shears. He sees the concept as a form of 'living history', where new pieces sit alongside vintage, for the kitchen, scullery, broom cupboard, dining room, study, bathroom and garden.

Hendy bought the listed property - an eighteenth-century soda-bottling shop, subsequently a tailor's and a confectioner's - in 2008, and restored it over three years with an uncompromising eye for authentic detail. His styling of each room is constantly evolving, creating beautiful scenes that reinvent history and make a relevant and compelling proposition for today's market, from a 1920s shopfront to a Victorian laundry room. Hendy's aim is to offer a unique shopping experience with old-fashioned customer service, in the manner of a traditional family-run department store, where the customer can explore the products on offer and then linger for a bite to eat.

'The shop is like a story book, taking the customer on a journey. Its dust jacket is the dark frontage and windows, opening into paragraphs of rooms that weave a narrative. Seeing customers place their purchases on the counter for wrapping, it's as though they've been on an adventure and these are their tales.'
- Alastair Hendy

Address
36 High Street, Hastings,
East Sussex, TN34 3ER, UK
Website
www.aghendy.com
Founder
Alastair Hendy

69

The beautiful renovation
of this characterful venue
encourages customers to
explore curated rooms and
vignettes on several floors.

PUSH

The thoughtful presentation
of the many products includes
using all surfaces, alcoves,
walls and even the sink.

Almost every delightful object displayed in the shop is for sale - even the vintage grocery-store equipment and other found treasures.

Every detail has been
considered, and vintage
and modern touches combine
to ensure a memorable and
satisfying shopping experience.

TIPS
· · · · · · ·

TIP 1 - We all love to make our own discoveries and find treasures with which we feel a special connection. Celebrate this with thoughtful, intricate and intriguing displays.

· · · · · · · ·

TIP 2 - Encourage your customers to journey through your space by thinking in terms of contained scenes and themed displays that place your products in context.

· · · · · · ·

TIP 3 - As e-commerce removes the chance of serendipitous browsing and sensory encounters, a beautifully presented shop can be appreciated more than ever as a source of inspiration and ideas.

The atmospheric rooms feel as though the occupier has just stepped out, leaving the visitor free to look around.

LE COMPTOIR GÉNÉRAL
PARIS, FRANCE
...

An oasis in the heart of the city, the destination venue Le Comptoir Général began life as a quirky hospitality venture, first and foremost a restaurant and bar with an energetic programme of cultural events running alongside. At its heart, the concept involves enabling guests to discover new and exotic world cultures through a variety of talks, performances, art, music and - perhaps most importantly - food and drink.

As the concept developed, more and more visitors asked for souvenirs of the experience to take home. Since the organizers were collaborating with an inspirational network of local and native producers for their cultural programme, they naturally also had access to a magnificent range of producers and purveyors of unusual produce. A complementary retail proposition was developed, and has since taken on a life of its own.

The space is large and curious in style, a feast for the eyes with mismatched furniture, furnishings, pictures, plants, curiosities and knick-knacks scattered carefully across tastefully faded nooks and scenes. Almost everything is for sale, either individually or through themed pop-ups that set up shop around the venue.

To steer these pop-ups and the merchandise in general, the founders hire 'treasure hunters' to scour the globe for quirky and exotic souvenirs of all shapes and sizes that will appeal to the diverse audience who flow through the doors. These experts - all of them in varied and unexpected walks of life, from fashion stylists to zoologists and explorers - ensure that the venue is constantly full of new ideas and objects to discover.

'The goods we are selling in our store are often handcrafted, fairly priced, organic and so on. But we don't stress that. The only way to build sustainable fair trade is to tell people they are just buying the best, coolest, strangest goods on earth!'
- Aurélien Laffon

Address
80 quai de Jemmapes, 75010 Paris, France
Website
www.lecomptoirgeneral.com
Founders
Aurélien Laffon, Céline Degrave,
Amah Ayivi and Guillaume Truttmann

Any style goes, from kitsch to colonial, 1950s retro to Caribbean beach hut, with a feeling of bringing outdoor living indoors.

TIPS

. . . .

TIP 1 - Whether your space is big or small, you can style an environment that customers want to spend time in. Make it welcoming with plenty of personal touches.

. . . .

TIP 2 - Allow customers to savour the atmosphere and linger, and give them space to explore. If they find pleasure in the experience, they are more likely to want to buy a souvenir of their visit.

. . . .

TIP 3 - Encourage the joy of serendipitous, treasured discoveries by displaying only a couple of each product at any time. But be sure to replenish regularly, so that everyone can benefit.

Almost everything in this eclectic establishment is for sale, presented as souvenirs for the charmed visitor to take away.

A background in sociology, anthropology and visual merchandizing gave Baylor Chapman a curiosity about how people use and enjoy spaces and the environment around them. She now applies her awareness of this to her celebrated plant-design business and shop, bringing nature into the heart of the city and into her customers' living spaces. Chapman's studio and shop, within the plot of the Stable Cafe in the Mission district of San Francisco, are accommodated in a sunroom and shipping container, but her intricate designs and displays spread throughout the café and its outdoor courtyard. The resulting oasis is juxtaposed with the surrounding industrial, concrete neighbourhood, forming a niche of lush green. It has become renowned as a place of tranquility, escape and inspiration, and visitors travel from far and wide to explore the variety of scenes that Chapman has carefully created through simple displays that combine vintage objects, salvaged materials and plenty of fresh, delicate greenery.

The sunroom at the heart of the site provides a photogenic indoor showroom with a citrus tree and an enormous hearth as its focal points. A contrasting forest of moss baskets hangs overhead. Linked to it is the shipping container, which was once the shopfront for the business but has now been outgrown and is used predominantly as Chapman's studio workspace. Outside, spilling across the courtyard, are displays and interventions of all shapes and sizes, providing little nooks and corners of discovery. Inspiring on a big and small scale, they provide something to suit the pocket and aspiration of every customer.

'No matter the size of a living space, you can bring a little bit of green inside. That's the idea I'm selling when I create my displays here: whether it's an elaborate living centrepiece or a tiny single succulent, there is something perfect for everyone to discover and take home.'
- Baylor Chapman

Address
2128 Folsom Street, San Francisco, CA 94110, USA
Website
www.lilabdesign.com
Founder
Baylor Chapman

The indoor-outdoor shop is overflowing with creative ideas for the display of greenery in any situation.

TIPS

. . . .

TIP 1 - Use your products to create compelling scenes, hidden treasure troves and intriguing sight lines, to draw customers through the space on a journey of discovery.

. . . .

TIP 2 - A retail space doesn't have to look traditional. As long as your products are displayed in a way that does them justice, thinking beyond the usual solutions will give you an appealing edge.

. . . .

TIP 3 - If space allows, create breathing room among your product displays, so that your customers can simply absorb the atmosphere, your offering and the pleasure you take in your business.

Visitors are encouraged to spend time among the scenic, landscaped displays, which combine the atmosphere of shop, café and public garden.

BLESS HOME
BERLIN, GERMANY
...

The BLESS label is renowned as a creative enigma: part fashion brand, part design house and part experimental art studio. Perhaps unsurprisingly, then, BLESS HOME takes a similarly rebellious approach to traditional retail, housing its flagship in a private apartment overlooking a quiet courtyard in central Berlin. Accessed by ringing the bell, the space is open three days a week and the rest of the time by appointment only.

The founders, Desiree Heiss and Ines Kaag, wanted to challenge the expectations of conventional sales of their designs by placing the products in a real, lived-in context, representing a complete lifestyle to be explored and unpacked by the visitor. In this house of artful style, everything is on display, and almost everything for sale - from the garments and accessories draped in the doorways to the furniture, bed linen, books and homewares piled on tables, stools, windowsills and floor. The decor is refreshed constantly, and new products are brought in regularly from the BLESS studio, although the fashion side of the business follows a more traditional seasonal schedule.

Looking after the space is a revolving team of 'house-sitters', who not only manage the shop and style the displays, but also live there. Each individual might inhabit the apartment for a few months (some live there longer) before handing over to the next. It's an unusual role in retail, one more akin to that of a performance artist: the sitters must be relaxed about having guests at any time, and comfortable with their entire life being on display, to be unpacked and perhaps purchased.

'Of course there are objects that grow close to my heart, so when they are sold it can be tough to say goodbye. However, with the knowledge that more beautiful things will follow, I enjoy giving away the pieces into enthusiastic hands.'
- BLESS 'house-sitter'

Address
Oderbergerstraße 60, 10435 Berlin, Germany
Website
www.bless-service.de
Founders
Desiree Heiss and Ines Kaag

The carefully chosen 'house-sitters' must deal with customers and arrange the displays, while also living in the apartment.

TIPS

. . . .

TIP 1 - Style your shop to tell a story about the world in which your products thrive. Show how you want your products to live on, after they are bought.

. . . .

TIP 2 - Create an inspirational setting and surprising encounters for your visitors by bringing unexpected features into your shop to encourage curiosity and offer a memorable visit.

. . . .

TIP 3 - Who says your shop should simply sell your product range? Keep its style fresh by using flexible furnishings and selling them on when you change the display.

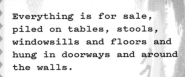

Everything is for sale, piled on tables, stools, windowsills and floors and hung in doorways and around the walls.

During her work as an exhibition curator for a number of Russian artists, the entrepreneur Ksenia Nunis regularly witnessed how challenging it is for new talent to break into the Russian art market. So she opened DEPST, her lower-ground-floor retail concept in Moscow, as a 'creative department store', with the aim of providing a welcoming, nurturing environment in which to showcase emerging Russian artists and help them to learn about the commercial world. She sees it as facilitating communication between people who love creating and appreciative audiences who have an insatiable appetite for visual beauty.

Nunis curates the eclectic, flexible, colourful environment to appeal to a range of pockets and tastes - from minimalist to kitsch - and stocks objects in many categories, from furniture to jewellery. She creates most of the quirky displays herself, but also allocates areas in which individual artists and designers can create their own displays, under her guidance, as part of the lively and theatrical scene.

The flexible space also accommodates exhibitions, and the ethos is one of total freedom and openness to collaboration of all types. A collaboration with the design outfit A-2-O Studio on a range of signature wrapping papers for customers' purchases, for example, proved popular, and the project will be repeated with other partners.

Nunis considers her staff to be one of the most important elements in the success of her store. They are passionate and knowledgeable about the products, and promote a friendly and happy attitude that encourages customers to feel at home. She values this form of communication above all others as she strives to create a place where people choose to linger, learn and discover.

'I love that the flexibility of our shop format means that we can showcase and sell any kind of product. There is basically no limit in style or category. It can be clothes, it can be furniture, and sometimes even exhibitions. We have total freedom and the openness to embrace any collaboration.'
- Ksenia Nunis

Address
Building 1, Tsvetnoy Boulevard 15,
Moscow 127051, Russia
Website
www.depst.ru
Founder
Ksenia Nunis
Wrapping paper design
A-2-O Studio (www.a-2-o.ru)

The shop floor is treated as a 'creative playground', scattered with eclectic installations and experimental display units.

TIPS
·······

TIP 1 - Bring the energy and anticipation of the world of the art gallery into your space by devising installations and inspirational settings that create a changing landscape for constant exploration.

·······

TIP 2 - Your shop shouldn't simply present your products. Tell a compelling story by bringing in your inspiration and other objects that you love, to set a personal scene.

·······

TIP 3 - Break with tradition and experiment with mixing a range of display methods, inventing your own solutions with found items, to style a creative playground that is full of fresh ideas.

Gift-wrapping is a key part of the service, using specially designed limited-edition papers.

The furnishing-design business of the creative duo Celia Montoya and Kike Keller began at home, where friends would often request versions of the one-off experimental homewares or furniture pieces that Keller designed and crafted for the couple's own house. Demand grew rapidly through word of mouth, and eventually the pair created a commercial home from home in an old sewing shop. This rambling space offers plenty of scope for displaying prototypes of the pieces that Montoya and Keller develop, and of which visitors can commission their own versions by choosing their preferred size, colour and finish.

This personal collection on an ever-expanding scale is combined with carefully curated exhibits and pieces by other artists and designers, from bespoke furnishings to custom motorbikes displayed as works of art on the wall. Keller and Montoya focus not on creating or curating collections that fit current trends, but rather on what they like, and on designs with personality.

Having been only simply refurbished, to retain the character of the historic building, the relaxed, experimental 'retail gallery' is constantly reworked. Visitors can buy into the ambience either through commissioning a product or by having a drink at the stylish bar. Each object,

piece of furniture and artwork is celebrated individually, with vignettes created around it - and the owners are always looking for fresh inspiration and talent to bring in, to ensure that their patrons discover something different on every visit.

'The whole building is our shop. Everything you see here is for sale. All the pieces are prototypes, which are available to be made on request. The best thing we have discovered with our space is that people like to enjoy design and creativity while also enjoying a drink.'
- Celia Montoya

Address
Calle Corredera Baja de San Pablo 17,
28004 Madrid, Spain
Website
www.kikekeller.com
Founders
Celia Montoya and Kike Keller

The venue is full of
intricate vignettes, showing
the made-to-order furniture
in context.

TIPS
. . . .

TIP 1 - For many customers, there is no thrill quite like that of finding a one-off treasure and taking it home. Such buyers will embrace an environment in which every detail is different.

. . . .

TIP 2 - Help your customers to visualize the world into which they are buying when they snap up one of your products. For maximum impact, style every piece within its own story.

. . . .

TIP 3 - If your products are unique and made to order, ensure that each customer leaves with plenty of inspiration, excited about welcoming their very own piece into their home.

Seasonally themed artworks mingle with the displays, so there is always something new to see.

Chapter 4 . Chapter

CRAFT & PROCESS
...

OPEN UP THE MAKING PROCESS OF YOUR PRODUCTS, TO BUILD EMOTIVE CONNECTIONS AND A STRONGER APPRECIATION OF QUALITY, SKILL AND EFFORT.
...

'Nothing should be made by man's labour which is not worth making'
- William Morris, 1884

The ever-expanding commercial landscape - and, more specifically, the boom in online retailing, with its endless array of options and sources - is sparking a strong reflex among consumers. While both the democracy of the internet and the evolving structure of physical shop leasing have certainly had the positive effect of enabling many more people to try their hand at the art of shopkeeping, the fact remains that all informed consumers will eventually navigate their way to those retail propositions with the most authenticity, the most compelling narratives and the most pleasing clarity of purpose.

As we become more savvy about the lack of joy in bad purchases and poor product offerings, a refreshing and welcome consumer movement is burgeoning. A lack of perceived authenticity or soul - which can be experienced when goods are too easily come by, with little effort and at too small a price, and without any kind of backstory to account for their making - is leading to an ever-increasing demand for process-led encounters. The desire to 'meet the maker' is strong.

While such encounters can still be online, a direct connection to and understanding of the origins of the product offering is key. Consumers want a proposition with a clear, accessible, human story that adds value to its *raison d'être*. This increasing desire to see how things are made, who made them, where, why and in what context is fuelling an exciting and welcome resurgence in independent shopkeeping. By its very nature, a maker-led retail proposition is scalable only to a certain extent, and that is its great appeal to the consumer. It guarantees a purchasing experience with meaning, delight and genuine satisfaction for all concerned.

Customers want to buy the 'real thing', the one-off, and ideally be involved actively in some way with the making itself - not necessarily hands-on, but at least as a witness. In this context, the story of the product is as valuable to the customer as the object itself; the latter is the souvenir of the experience, a memento of the story into which they have bought. For the shopkeeper, the joy and reward are in the appreciation of their craft, the recognition of the time and effort they have put into honing a skill, and the ability to control every aspect of the story they tell. A physical shop - whether permanent or transient - enables face-to-face encounters with and direct feedback from the audience, allowing the shopkeeper to nurture and develop a stronger business and product offering. Overall, bringing the craft process - or at least those elements that it is practical to reveal in a public space - into the heart of the shop is compelling, and guarantees more memorable encounters.

In his utopian manifesto *News From Nowhere* (1890), the English designer and writer William Morris wrote of the 'workshops of craftsmen returning to

street corners across the city', an idealized vision that was a direct response to the negative social and cultural effects of the Industrial Revolution. But the dream that Morris described in the nineteenth century can now be seen in the contemporary movement that is examined in this chapter: an intelligent and emotional response to the 'new Industrial Revolution' and the often impersonal encounters of our digitally powered age. In fact, the concept of the 'workshop' itself has pleasing relevance to this movement, too, having originated at a time when craftsmen worked in and sold from the same space - usually a room in their house. Today the activity may not be carried out in the craftsman's home - although many start their businesses at the kitchen table - but a maker-led retail environment can create just such a compelling atmosphere.

Consumers increasingly want to buy for good, not simply for the sake of making a purchase, and to find more meaning and definition in a crowded marketplace. They also want to be more deeply involved in understanding the journey the product makes to the shelf: to be taught, and to learn. The concept of 'lifelong learning' as a way to enrich modern lifestyles is more popular than ever before, and retail propositions that integrate authentic and beneficial education are hot property.

The maker-led retail approach offers an ideal scenario for meeting this demand. In exposing customers to a meaningful product and the opportunity to broaden their horizons, be introduced to and appreciate new-found art forms and skills, and find satisfaction in investing in the businesses they encounter, it breathes an interesting new energy into the age-old concept of craft patronage. It also builds a stronger understanding of the product itself, which can only benefit the shopkeeper in the long term through the increased likelihood of repeat purchases, word-of-mouth referrals and greater investment.

To manage the role of shopkeeper
successfully alongside that of craftsman
requires a careful balance that combines
creative awareness of the audience's
experience with focused practicality.
This multi-skilled requirement magnifies
the complexity and the entrepreneurial
requirement of independent shopkeeping
today. It is therefore not without its
challenges, and recognition is due to
these shopkeepers for their graft and
dedication. For the craftsman-shopkeeper,
the rewards can of course be plentiful.
Demand from willing patrons is growing,
and more shopkeepers of this calibre
are vital to the continued growth of
an exciting and varied commercial scene.

Housed in a unit in the regenerated Strand Arcade, a cluster of boutiques dedicated to artisan retail businesses, Andrew McDonald's bespoke footwear workshop is a celebrated fixture of the independent retail scene in Sydney. McDonald has been a shoemaker since 1990, and when he opened his newest shop he set out to create a space that celebrates both the making and the selling, offering a tangible link to the craft process that is lost in much contemporary retail.

At the heart of McDonald's philosophy is a passionate belief in offering the finest handcrafted footwear for men and women by following a process that shuns modern-day mass production. Made in limited quantities, his shoes have a rustic, sculptural quality and a unique character, and these values are referenced throughout the shop. The honest, artisanal approach is reflected by a minimal window display, to allow a clear view into the shop, and is coupled with a simple, traditional external signboard overhead.

The compact space - low-lit and raw - reflects perfectly the strong statement of the handsome footwear, and merges display space and workspace so that visitors feel completely involved in understanding the process and sensations of the shoemaking experience, through watching, touching and smelling. Staying true to the brand's anti-mass-manufacturing ethos, the fixtures and fittings are all authentic and reclaimed, reinforcing the delightful personality and integrity, and telling a story of their own. Further visual communication is kept to a minimum, allowing the products to speak and enhancing the value of the personal, face-to-face service.

'I like to approach my space more as an interactive museum shop than as a retail mausoleum. I present my shoes as stories waiting to be told, waiting for the right person to pick them up, activate their story and take them on a journey.'
- Andrew McDonald

Address
121-25 The Strand Arcade (2nd floor),
412-14 George Street, Sydney,
NSW 2000, Australia
Website
www.andrewmcdonald.com.au
Founder
Andrew McDonald

Staying true to an anti-mass-manufacturing ethos, the shop's display fixtures are all reclaimed and cost-effective.

The shoemaking process involves making a last for each customer, and these are displayed as part of the visual storytelling.

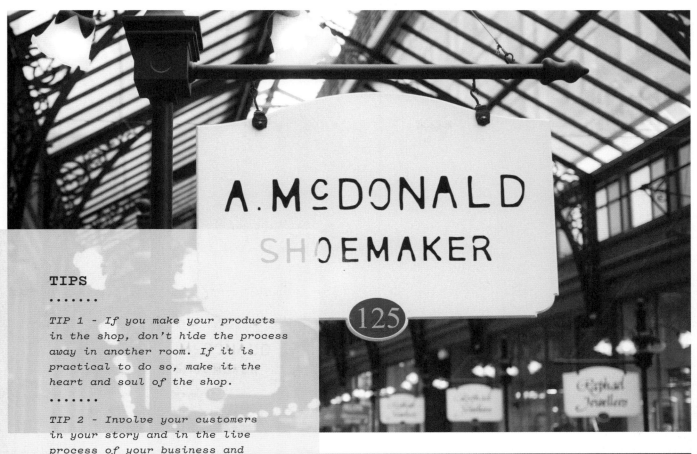

A. McDONALD
SHOEMAKER

125

TIPS

. . . .

TIP 1 - If you make your products in the shop, don't hide the process away in another room. If it is practical to do so, make it the heart and soul of the shop.

. . . .

TIP 2 - Involve your customers in your story and in the live process of your business and products. Independent retail success relies on nurturing an engaged community.

. . . .

TIP 3 - Before you invest in brand-new fixtures and fittings, think about whether reclaimed and vintage pieces could tell a better story that complements your authentic production process.

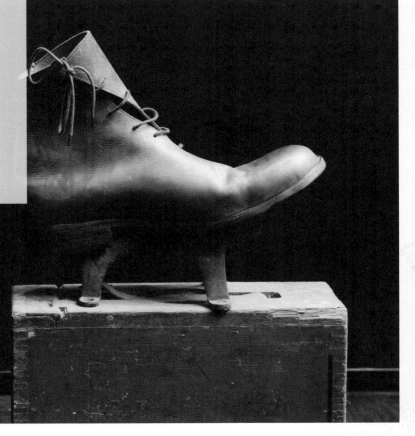

CUT BROOKLYN
BROOKLYN, USA
...

Joel Bukiewicz is a rare breed of maker - one of very few craftsmen outside the famous Japanese workshops to be devoted to making exquisite steel kitchen knives completely by his own hand. He sells his wares from an immaculate storefront workshop space that combines hints of nostalgic Americana with an industrial precision that reflects the very highest quality of modern workmanship.

Bukiewicz's business evolved organically after he took some time off from a fledgling writing career to explore new skills, and quickly discovered a talent that resulted in a word-of-mouth waiting list for his pieces. The shop is thriving, and his knives have a cult following of amateur and professional cooks alike. His craft-led operation proves that quality not quantity can build a solid business, and customers are willing to wait months to receive a made-to-order blade, to ensure that it is made personally by him.

One of the most impressive qualities of the business is Bukiewicz's refusal to bow to commercial demand and scale up, which would inevitably dilute the promise of the product. The workshop is open only two days a week to direct customers, and the knives available for purchase that week are displayed on a single magnetic strip, framed on one wall of the workshop.

A photo of this knife display is also posted to the Cut website and social media feeds, for Bukiewicz's audience of international fans to covet. Then the buying begins. Up to fifteen knives are available each week - each one unique - and when they are gone, they are gone.

'There's a consumer shift happening where people want to educate themselves about food and products and see it all happening. I'm so fortunate to be sitting at the convergence of the handmade and food worlds.'
- Joel Bukiewicz

Address
461 3rd Avenue, Brooklyn, NY 11215, USA
Website
www.cutbrooklyn.com
Founder
Joel Bukiewicz

TIPS
. . . .

TIP 1 - If you are a maker, you know that honed skills like yours don't appear overnight. Where you can, communicate this to your customers through demonstration rather than explanation.

. . . .

TIP 2 - Increasingly, customers want to buy products that have an inspiring and personal story. Make that story as visible as possible - it is a valuable asset.

. . . .

TIP 3 - If you make your own products, celebrate the fact that perfecting them takes time. Don't feel the pressure to have too many pieces on show. Quality, not quantity, is compelling.

The knife display blackboard is the focal point of the shop, framed by a warm and vibrant red-painted wall.

Craftsmanship is celebrated in every detail of the shop, such as the wooden signage, which features the logo.

TORTUS
COPENHAGEN, DENMARK
...

The small but perfectly formed ceramic workshop Tortus punches far above its weight. With a limited output of beautiful handmade ceramic pieces that are coveted the world over, and a communications strategy based on opening up the making process both physically and through social media, the brand is drawing an ever-growing audience of admirers from around the globe. Dedicated to presenting a modern adaptation of traditional and time-tested methods, the business holds true to an ethos built on the appreciation of the slow yet steady creature after which the workshop is named - moving at its own humble pace and respecting the materials and rituals of ceramic work.

Founded by Eric Landon, a graduate of the Danish School of Design in Copenhagen, the studio recognizes a responsibility to preserve the craft of a centuries-old Danish tradition. That is why each Tortus piece is handmade in the city-centre studio, in time-honoured tradition, without exception. Increasing demand is, however, necessitating ever more hands in the studio, so the team is being expanded carefully to allow larger-scale production while retaining the promise of artisanal quality and nurturing a new generation of potters.

The beautiful space houses both the workshop and an informal display area for the latest pieces. It also acts as a picturesque backdrop for the many videos and pieces of social media content that the studio's team produces for its ever-growing worldwide audience, who follow their output and development avidly online. The venue also hosts classes and events, welcoming audiences into the brand's home and the heart of the business, and ensuring a personal touch to the experience.

'The internet and social media give small, holistic producers like us a louder voice, and our audience is no longer local, like those of the makers of the past. It is global, and we can share our story every day with the click of a mouse.'
- Eric Landon

Address
Kompagnistræde 23, 1208 Copenhagen, Denmark
Website
www.tortus-copenhagen.com
Founder
Eric Landon

Tortus's founder, Eric Landon, at work in the studio, with some of his part-finished creations on display behind.

TIPS

. . . .

TIP 1 - Consider inviting your customers directly into your workspace, rather than setting up a separate shop. Buying from the source makes a purchase more memorable, emotive and personal.

. . . .

TIP 2 - Keep your displays simple, and allow space for each piece to breathe, so that the focus is on the individual skill and style - especially if each product you make is different.

. . . .

TIP 3 - Don't dress the space to impress just because you have visitors. Keep things authentic, simple and stylish, and let the live activity and resulting products do the talking.

The studio offers a much-praised experience in the heart of the city, and exudes a feeling of calm creativity.

The entrepreneurial self-taught designers and leather craftswomen Mariel Gonzalez and Alexa Schoorl set up their collaborative shop with the aim of making beautiful, high-quality and useful leather products. They wanted to offer an environment in which their customers would feel welcomed into the workshop process, witness the pieces being made and then make informed purchases complete with the much-desired authentic product story.

The pair's approach to their 'storefront studio' is informal and friendly, reflecting their own home environments, with lots of plants and personal touches such as found treasures and paintings from friends on the walls. A big, sunny, uncluttered window ensures plenty of natural light and a feel-good atmosphere.

The studio is an open space with a big work table in full view behind the counter of the cosy shop. This is the heart of the space, where the activity of the business is played out each day, and it benefits from the bright, airy shopfront as well as forming a focal point from the street. Each of the finished products on display is given equal attention, with its own dedicated display shelf, niche or wall hook, presented in a relaxed, tactile style among the foliage. A simple set-up of scaffolding bar and hooks is used in the window to display a changing selection of the latest finished pieces.

The business is growing fast, and Gonzalez and Schoorl are expanding. They have taken on more space, moving their increasing production to the back and upstairs, to leave room for a bigger studio and shop.

'We are learning and improving our skills all the time. Good vibes in the studio are very important to us, and our customers feel this directly when they visit. They love the smell when they walk in, the plants, and getting to see the studio where everything is made.'
- Mariel Gonzalez

Address
1130 College Street, Toronto, ON,
M6H 1B6, Canada
Website
www.eleventhirtyshop.com
Founders
Mariel Gonzalez and Alexa Schoorl

Each finished product is displayed in its own space on shelves or ceiling and wall hooks, across the sunny shop.

TIPS

· · · · · · ·

TIP 1 - Don't be shy: open up glimpses into the workings of your business and your craft. Your customers will appreciate seeing and understanding more of the world into which they are buying.

· · · · · · ·

TIP 2 - Blend your retail space with your studio or workshop and involve your customers in the conversations, where appropriate. You'll build a stronger following and word-of-mouth support.

· · · · · · ·

TIP 3 - Don't underestimate the value to your business of opening up your process: listen to and learn from your customers in a live, welcoming, hands-on environment.

The whole creative process is on view, and visitors are welcomed in and encouraged to get involved in the conversation.

GOOD & PROPER TEA
LONDON, UK
...

The tea connoisseur Emilie Holmes's successfully crowdfunded business Good & Proper Tea - which began life at her kitchen table - is now opening permanent outlets in London, supported by a booming online shop to reach a wider audience. But for the first five years the business revolved around the website and a beautifully converted silver Citroën H van from 1974 - fitted with work surfaces, water tanks, a boiler, a fridge, display shelves and plenty of storage, and a line of customized brewing stations on the counter - which allowed Emilie to travel far and wide with a self-contained proposition to demonstrate the art of brewing good tea.

Each takeaway tea is brewed to order for a maximum of three minutes in a glass teapot, while the customer watches the countdown on a timer next to their pot. This makes the craft process tangible and an important part of the service experience. The brewing stations are now a popular, permanent feature of all G&PT outlets.

Complemented by home-made cakes and crumpets, and selling a variety of loose-leaf teas for brewing at home, the offering has gained a strong following and is putting tea firmly on the map as an alternative to the artisan coffee trend. The characterful, eye-catching van makes regular appearances at food markets, as well as touring to special events and summer festivals. And, because weather notably affects the business, one of a number of innovative service elements that Emilie has introduced is a pre-ordering system via Twitter, so that regulars can collect their tea and go, without having to wait in the rain.

'In the van, I like everything to be very clean and neat. It needs to look cosy from the outside to invite passers-by to want a warming cup of tea - but also clean and minimal to cue quality. I love being in there with the radio on, setting up.'
- Emilie Holmes

Address
96A Leather Lane, London EC1N 7TX, UK
Website
www.goodandpropertea.com
Founder
Emilie Holmes

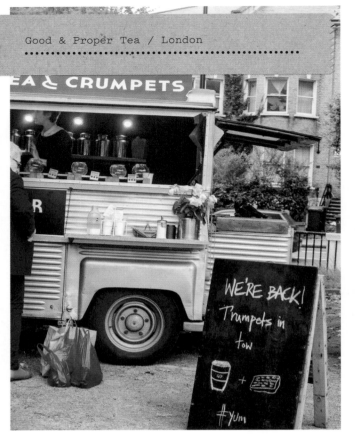

The charming van has allowed founder Emilie Holmes to transport her tea across the United Kingdom and Europe.

TIPS

. . . .

TIP 1 - If the enjoyment of your product can be enhanced by the way in which the customer uses it, don't just tell them - show them or serve them in the way that you recommend.

. . . .

TIP 2 - Wheels or no wheels, be true to your own style. Determine what your set-up should do and where you want to be seen, then define your method.

. . . .

TIP 3 - Think about the details. These little things show the craft of your process and the care and attention to detail you bring to it because it is your life's work.

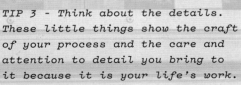

In a warehouse in the historic Brooklyn Navy Yard, this award-winning independent distillery originated from the experiments of its co-founder, Colin Spoelman, in distilling moonshine and bourbon as a hobby in his apartment. When it launched in 2010, it was the first whiskey distillery in New York City since Prohibition (1920-33).

The rapidly expanding venue, now spread across three buildings, houses the factory and barrel room, a shop, a tasting room, a cocktail bar and a museum space called the Boozeum - not to mention what is claimed to be the best lavatory in Brooklyn. The firm sees the focus of the visitor experience as being less on commerce - although it has a strong wholesale business - and more on being a friendly and open-minded destination that prioritizes education, whiskey appreciation, history and fun.

At first, the shop was simply a tasting room where visitors could sample and then purchase the whiskey, but it has diversified into explaining the making process and how the distillery's whiskeys are different. It also serves samples of experimental whiskeys that are not yet available to buy, as a great way of testing future products and gaining valuable feedback.

These informal samples are presented in an eclectic selection of bottles with handwritten labels, and a team member is always ready with an anecdote or two up their sleeve. For the team, who admit that making good whiskey is not easy, being able to step back and share the product and their stories with an appreciative audience helps them to keep perspective and fuels their desire to continue exploring and making a better product.

'To have a store where our bottles are prominent reinforces the fact that everything about our whiskey is different from what people have tried before. We have very simple packaging, so people know that our efforts go into what's in the bottle, not what's on the bottle.'
- Colin Spoelman

Address
299 Sands Street, Building 121, Brooklyn, NY 11205, USA
Website
www.kingscountydistillery.com
Founders
Colin Spoelman and David Haskell

The barrel room is on view next to the shop and restaurant, demonstrating that the products are truly made in Brooklyn.

TIPS

......

TIP 1 - Don't be shy about sharing your work in progress with your customers, and asking for feedback. They will appreciate your trust and feel a more personal connection with your brand.

......

TIP 2 - There is no need to dress your works in progress as if they were finished products. Honesty is a strong selling point and an important part of your story.

......

TIP 3 - If you want to nurture your customers for the long term, invite them in to learn about your story so far. Hands-on experiences are the most memorable.

Various distilling experiments under way and on display, for tasting sessions and feedback from loyal customers.

EDIT & ABUNDANCE

CONSIDER WHETHER YOUR BRAND
BETTER SUITS AN EDITED SELECTION
AND A RAREFIED PROMISE, OR THE
JOY ASSOCIATED WITH ABUNDANT CHOICE.

...

*'Goods are displayed by thousands of
shopkeepers with a sense of beauty
that finds no other outlet.'*
- Mignon McLaughlin, 1950s

As we saw briefly in Chapter Two, the
thrilling sense of potential offered by a
wealth of options has long been compelling
for customers. Nurturing the feeling of
opportunity, the joy of discovery and the
freedom to make a different purchase from
the next person all count for a lot when
a shopkeeper is considering how to shape
a retail experience.

Customers thrive on the opportunity of
variety, but not on the confusion of volume.
The desire to feel empowered to make
a satisfying purchase has a great deal
of influence on where and how consumers
choose to shop, and freedom of choice
is certainly key to this. However, in
a frenetic modern marketplace in which
consumers are faced with never-ending
options and the unappealing saturation
of over-production - sometimes referred
to as the 'age of super-abundance' - there
is also an increasing desire to be guided
through the options available, and for
ways to reduce the graft of filtering
through the good, the bad and the ugly

to discover the 'treasure' that we know must be there somewhere.

Increasingly, the style of shop in which a customer chooses to spend precious time does not involve the delivery of goods in a practical sense, but rather surprises and delights its audience with the unexpected, the thoughtful and the new ideas that enhance and nurture our lifestyles.

We have seen that customers enjoy the sensation of seeking, and want to be able to make their own decisions, but that they also crave support in making sense of this modern landscape of choice. Expert guidance can help them to understand what is inherently important, what is of short-term relevance and what is irrelevant or not worthy of attention and money.This has resulted in the popularity of the twenty-first-century ideas of curation and the 'concept store', which have taken our retail scene by storm, both online and on our streets. But the definition of this and the most effective approaches to it can be lost in the enthusiasm of the opportunity.

As the acclaimed curator and visionary Hans Ulrich Obrist has described in his public talks, and touched on in his book *A Brief History of Curating* (2008), the contemporary practice of curation draws on specific historic functions of the role, namely the sharing of knowledge, research and the ability to 'display and arrange'. Notably, and of most relevance to the retail environment, he explains that the curator selects and arranges to 'add value'. Ultimately, the shopkeeper is a curator, defining a narrative and reasoning around the collection of goods they choose to offer to their audience. This notion can be promoted to a greater or lesser extent, and varies in style from category to category, but in general, honing the art of contemporary shopkeeping revolves around an understanding of the techniques and psychology of curation.

Through curation, the shopkeeper shapes their own lifestyle story or cultural viewpoint, aiming to create a compelling atmosphere and scene into which they

invite their audience. Success comes through balancing their vision with the aspirations of their audience, to ensure an effective and successful proposition into which customers will wish to buy. In some cases the audience will naturally find the retail concept that rings most true with their own values, and in other cases the shopkeeper will choose to respond to an existing demand, niche or target audience, and create a relevant context accordingly.

As social animals, humans want both to be valued as individuals and to fit into the pack. The cultural weight that is given to commercial trends - the notion of setting a direction in fashion or food, for example - is testament to the consumer's need for self-expression and new stimulation, combined with a clarity of thinking and explanation that ensures we feel secure in our choices. So again, in a retail context, by introducing experts and arbiters of taste to steer the audience's shopping decisions, a proposition will meet the demand for both individual outcomes and the satisfaction of making a good purchase.

Curation within the retail environment does not necessarily mean cutting down or limiting the products on display, although it does certainly mean editing out the bad options. In essence, it means that the presence of each product must be justified and its *raison d'être* made clear. In the case of an abundance of product, a carefully considered display strategy must be employed that celebrates the options without allowing the experience to feel like a chaotic, unsatisfactory jumble with unclear outcomes or paths to purchase.

The skill of presenting multiple products and nurturing the customer's desire for excitement at the potential of choice while maintaining an overall considered order is one of the key arts of the shopkeeper, and takes dedication, experimentation and practice to perfect. It takes a rare instinct and acute awareness of the mindset of the customer to make it fly.

The shopkeeper must decide whether their

particular commercial proposition or product
suits an opulent approach to presentation,
or one that champions the appeal of
scarcity. Both require creative ingenuity
to ensure that the 'value' of the product
range is conveyed effectively. Whether the
chosen style of retailing celebrates the
joy and potential of abundance, or focuses
on the compelling feeling of exclusivity
inherent in gathering the fine and the
few, it will find a welcome audience. The
choice of approach is simply down to each
shopkeeper's story and vision, and success
relies on their dedication to honing the art
of contemporary commercial curation.

MORIOKA SHOTEN
TOKYO, JAPAN
...

This small bookshop and gallery in the Ginza district sells copies of a single title, chosen weekly by its owner, the long-time bookseller Yoshiyuki Morioka. The shop's name simply means Morioka's Bookshop, and it is described humbly as 'a single room with a single book'.

Before opening it, Morioka ran another bookshop for ten years, and there he stocked some 200 titles and organized several book launches each year. During these events, he noted that many people visited the shop for the sake of this single book, and so he started to believe that a bookshop could perhaps be managed with only one title at a time.

Morioka describes his concept as 'a bookshop that organizes an exhibition derived from a single book'. For example, when selling a book on flowers, the shop is transformed into a gallery celebrating a flower that appears in that book. Morioka asks the authors and editors to spend as much time as possible at the bookshop during the week of their exhibition, making the shop their workspace for that time.

The visual displays are simply and respectfully presented on the walls, in frames or with wires and clips. Furniture is kept to a minimum, with a statement vintage filing chest for payments, gift-wrapping and storage, and a single table displaying a few copies of the book. The window is kept clear - like that of an art gallery - to allow the contents of the shop to shine. A concise written explanation of the shop concept is placed simply on the glass in vinyl lettering.

'This is an attempt to make the two-dimensional book into a three-dimensional ambience and experience. I believe that my customers, or readers, should feel as though they are entering into the book itself.'
- Yoshiyuki Morioka

Address
Suzuki Building 1F, 1-28-15 Ginza,
Chuo-ku, Tokyo, Japan
Founder
Yoshiyuki Morioka
Designer
Takram (www.takram.com)

Only a few copies of the book are displayed, to give the feeling of exclusivity that is usually found in art galleries.

The space is kept completely flexible, so that it can be reinvented with simple furniture and details for each book that is launched. Nothing is fixed.

TIPS

·······

TIP 1 - Think about the essence of what you are selling and how you could present some of your ideas as a gallery of visual references, to enhance your storytelling.

·······

TIP 2 - If you have an impactful visual narrative running through the inside of your shop, don't confuse it by cluttering your windows. Simple vinyl works beautifully for a sophisticated touch.

·······

TIP 3 - Don't feel that you must cram your shop full of product. With smart storage, you can have plenty in stock while keeping your displays simple, focused and compelling.

The window is kept clear to allow the gallery-like shop to speak out to potential customers on its own terms, with just a simple explanation.

MORIOKA SHOTEN & CO., LTD.
A SINGLE ROOM WITH A SINGLE BOOK
SUZUKI BUILDING, 1-28-15 GINZA,
CHUO-KU, TOKYO, JAPAN

OBJECT_IFY 139
NEW YORK CITY, USA
···

After working in the world of art galleries, Maria Candanoza wanted to create a welcoming space of her own, somewhere between gallery and shop. So, since 2012 she has focused on creating and building a platform that enables young, emerging artists to sell their work in the big city. The physical shop itself closed in 2016, but the online shop lives on. Her aim has always been to create a platform that enables young, emerging artists to sell their work in the big city. Believing that art is for everyone, and that everyone should have the opportunity to own it and share it, Candanoza holds open submissions for artists, and intends the pieces she chooses to be accessible and affordable to a range of buyers.

The stylish space of the shop itself was pared-back and functional, making it completely flexible. In it, Candanoza curated new pieces and displays every couple of weeks, and hosted popular events twice a month to introduce new artists, authors and products. Space was limited, so tight curation within the range was important, as were smart storage and displays.

A very effective display feature was the Prints Wall, a floor-to-ceiling magnetic grid that gave the geometric impression of a cutting mat in a creative studio. New graphic works could quickly and flexibly be hung on it for maximum impact, and left no no marks when they were removed. This strong visual effect continues on the website, bringing a clear methodology to the way the works are presented. The Objects Wall used a smart modular peg system for ever-changing formations of product display, while sleek floating drawers on the opposite wall provided ample storage.

'The books and magazines section was a deliberately simple wall design inspired by a gallery, that could hold no more than fifty books. That way the selection was always limited and people could really engage with the work we were showing.'
- Maria Candanoza

Website
www.objectify139.com
Founder
Maria Candanoza

Whitewashed walls provided a welcoming, tactile backdrop for the colour-popping product displays and glowing neon signs.

TIPS

....

TIP 1 - If you have limited floor space for displays, explore ways of maximizing your walls for carefully presented edits. Use varying display methods to give each theme its own style.

....

TIP 2 - Use eye-catching title signage to help customers to navigate your product types or themes, then let the products do the talking within each theme.

....

TIP 3 - Following the lead of the art gallery, keep your backdrops simple to allow your product selections to pop. You don't have to go all-white, just keep things crisp, clean and clear.

The shop was long and narrow, with limited presentation space, but the selection of varied textures and different display techniques gave it a spacious and airy feel.

COTTONCAKE
AMSTERDAM,
THE NETHERLANDS
•••

With COTTONCAKE, Tessa van Herwijnen and Jorinde Westhoff - whose backgrounds are in psychology and communications respectively - set about making their dream come true. That dream was one of opening a shop where they could bring together everything they discovered, loved and brought back from their global travels, and introduce these ideas and finds to an appreciative audience. The outcome is part boutique and part café, and a beautifully executed example of the increasingly popular, highly edited 'concept store' format. It's a space where the duo happily learn by trial and error, and are steered creatively by their gut feelings.

The design of the space has an authentic, down-to-earth approach that is timeless and not tied to trends. The simple, rustic materials are submerged in thick layers of white paint so that the textures create an interesting backdrop and a sense of cleanliness and unity; colour comes only from the thoughtful selection of products on display, and from the fresh food that is served. Products are kept to a tight edit that presents just one or two of each, to enhance the value of the customer's choice.

As well as creating this minimalist edit, the duo intend the shop to be a space where visitors can feel at ease whiling away pleasurable time, so they are continuously collecting authentic furniture, furnishings and objects to make the place feel like a home. Delightful features include a working Faema espresso machine - much loved by customers and dating from 1961 - and a reclaimed farm workbench proudly placed in the centre of the shop, along with numerous tiny details such as wild found treasures scattered among the product displays.

'We love travelling and discovering - products that are designed with love; great food where you feel the passion of the person who prepared it. We wanted our shop to be our treasury, where we can collect all these things, and share them with others. We love to search without borders.'
- Jorinde Westhoff

Address
1e van der Helststraat 76-hs,
1072NZ Amsterdam, The Netherlands
Website
www.cottoncake.nl
Founders
Tessa van Herwijnen and Jorinde Westhoff

Colour and texture are used thoughtfully in everything from the wall displays to the food that is served.

TIPS

. . . .

TIP 1 - If your preferred style is a very tight edit, think about how the individual products sit alongside one another so that they are complementary rather than fighting for attention.

. . . .

TIP 2 - Keep your presentation sleek, displaying just one or two of each piece - but be sure to replenish. Focusing on fewer products allows the value of each to be appreciated.

. . . .

TIP 3 - Grouping different products in combinations of three is pleasing to the eye. Generally speaking, mix texture and scale, but not too many different colours in any one set.

Placing white furniture against a textured white background creates serenity and brings the colourful details to the foreground.

The influential destination concept store Merci in Paris was founded in 2009 by Bernard and Marie-France Cohen, with the aim of giving the city a place that brought together the best of fashion, design, art, lifestyle and food, in an immersive environment bursting with creative flair. Although they have since passed on the torch, the ethos and dedication to the art of retail as a cultural experience remains.

The shopper's experience is focused on a central, full-height atrium space, which sets the pace and tone. This main floor and the feature wall introduce an annual programme of large-scale installations, exploratory exhibitions and narrative themes, around which the product selection is tightly curated. Pieces by world-renowned designers sit alongside those by up-and-coming talents and one-off vintage pieces, presented in creative displays that use the full area and height of the space.

Themes are inspired by cultural events, current affairs and trends in design, literature, cooking and lifestyle. The aim is to encourage people to pause and think about the story that is being presented to them, as much as to make a purchase.

This honed level of product editing and scenic display techniques runs across every department, under the watchful eye of the artistic director, Daniel Rozensztroch. The aim is to create an overall feeling of abundance - of products, ideas and discoveries to be made - but at the same time to present an expert selection within any one category or theme, where each product is a treasure.

'I like to make people think. I want to inspire collective consciousness to motivate people to consider the everyday decisions they make, to move towards greater positivity and joy. The products people purchase can certainly help with that process, if we select and display the right ones.'

- Daniel Rozensztroch, artistic director

Address
111 Boulevard Beaumarchais,
75003 Paris, France
Website
www.merci-merci.com
Founders
Bernard and Marie-France Cohen

Earth, hand & fire

The curation pays particular attention to the volume of the space, taking advantage of its impressive ceiling height.

SLOW LIFE

KEEP COOL LIFE IS BEAUTIFUL

TIPS

. . . .

TIP 1 - If you have the space, think in multiples and at scale, to bring some installation art or theatre to your curation style. Shape your space in sweeping gestures.

. . . .

TIP 2 - Experiment with creating a big visual wall as the focal point to introduce each edit, and contain the product range on horizontal surfaces so that the eye can read it easily.

. . . .

TIP 3 - Explore how to use every surface - including ceiling and floor - to enhance the way you present your edit and make it an immersive experience that does justice to your products.

In this unusual space, the view from above is also considered and arranged so as to be pleasing to the eye.

MOKO MARKET
HELSINKI, FINLAND
...

Inspired by their wonderfully bohemian upbringing and the traditions of an eccentric country house, sisters Lilli and Susu Toukolehto opened their vibrant interior-design shop in 2006 with the vision of designing, making and sourcing homewares and furnishings to bring joy into every living space, on any scale. The shop has become a thriving meeting point and a source of colourful inspiration at the heart of its neighbourhood, attracting a creative community from far and wide. Its popular, homely cafe serves fresh home-made lunches in the middle of an ever-changing landscape of vibrant product displays.

Piled on every surface, in multiples and in every colour, the compelling wealth of products combines the pair's own design collections with high-quality furnishings from other makers. Pieces of vintage furniture are also for sale, contributing to an abundant offering that is embellished with a vast collection of smaller decorative objects from around the globe.

The spirited, opulently stocked space celebrates the serendipity and pleasure that are to be found in mismatched products and surprising combinations, and is deliberately opposed to the worldwide movement that currently favours highly edited, minimalist concept stores. The Toukolehtos pride themselves on curating 'organized creative chaos', with no set rules, but a clear and regimented system of stock-taking does underpin the business. Their approach ensures that there is a treasure for everyone to discover, with a multitude of options, choices and ideas presented at every turn, and focuses on nurturing strong feelings of optimism, passion and creative potential.

'We wanted to create something unique that would be totally our own - a special place with our personal touch. We did everything as we would have done in our own home. It's a place with lots of ideas, lots of activity and lots of happy people.'
- Lilli and Susu Toukolehto

Address
Perämiehenkatu 10, 00150 Helsinki, Finland
Website
www.moko.fi
Founders
Lilli and Susu Toukolehto

The large number of products
on display are choreographed
in simple patterns to help the
eye to navigate.

TIPS

....

TIP 1 - If an opulent volume of product is your style, embrace and celebrate the clash of textures, colours, shapes and scales. If you do it, do it with conviction.

....

TIP 2 - Piled high and covering every surface, displays still need a creative eye to prevent them from looking a mess. Pay attention to the details, patterns and alignments in the mix.

....

TIP 3 - A wealth of options encourages a sense of joy and anticipation in the buyer, but can also bring confusion and frustration. Create patterns that bring order, and draw the eye to explore.

Displaying an eclectic range of products need not be chaotic, and can help to encourage a sense of anticipation.

GEKAAPT
AMSTERDAM, THE NETHERLANDS
•••

One of the original and most renowned pop-up concepts in Amsterdam, Gekaapt was the brainchild of three young entrepreneurs who - all simply looking for an outlet from which to sell their own products, at first - decided in 2013 to combine their passions into a single temporary retail offering. This first shop very quickly gained a reputation for high quality and a great atmosphere, and other local independent brands rapidly wanted to become part of it. So Gekaapt was born.

A few years later, and still with no fixed abode, this much-loved pop-up continues to appear every few months, growing in scale all the time. In between it lives simply as a Facebook page with a strong word-of-mouth following.

The retail model is collaborative, and brands and individual designers constantly apply to become part of the mix. The growing network of talent ensures that plenty of creative, styling and business expertise is always available to make the store activations operate at their best.

The team opens a new space with a new story every three to six months, in an empty unit somewhere in the city. The huge amount of support and experience that rallies around means that they can set up shop in just two or three days.

Notably, there are no official employees. Gekaapt is run collaboratively by the owners and makers of the brands and products it sells. Each brand retains its own values and narrative within the space, but all are connected by a love of high-quality produce, good stories and making a difference through bringing great people together.

'In the beginning we were just a bunch of young entrepreneurs trying to make a concept store out of an empty space. We started with seven brands, but within a month we had twenty-two brands wanting to join our shop. We never thought that would happen!'
- Aanyoung Yeh

Address
Various locations, Amsterdam, The Netherlands
Website
www.facebook.com/gekaapt
Founders
Rick Ruijter, Jan Swinkels and Aanyoung Yeh

TIPS
. . . .

TIP 1 - Even with a broad selection
of products and wide curation,
every object can have its home
within the space. Take time to
give each its moment of attention.

. . . .

TIP 2 - Think on many levels:
not just shelves, but landscaped
levels across the space. This helps
the eye to break up the mass of
options, and digest each in turn.

If your shop is a busy bustle of different products, create a high point for the payment desk so that your customers can locate you freely and without confusion.

Multiples of an item are effective when presented together, becoming props within the set design of the shop.

Vary your display surfaces to create a landscape that keeps the eye interested and encourages the customer to scan for treasures.

STAGING & SCENERY

...

CREATE IMMERSIVE SCENES FOR YOUR PRODUCTS, TO GIVE THEM AN INSPIRING AND EXPLANATORY CONTEXT THAT CAPTURES THE IMAGINATION.

...

'People don't buy for logical reasons. They buy for emotional reasons.'
- Zig Ziglar (1926-2012)

The retail environment is increasingly focused on facilitating enjoyment and inspiration, and as the American writer Zig Ziglar stressed catering to the emotions, through selling ideas and aspirational vision. It is about entertainment and immersion - a form of 'theatre', indeed, as is so often said.

In today's market almost anything can be found with speed and ease, in more and more cases through online interaction. For that reason we now seek, more than ever, visual stimulation and physical interaction - and not just the final act of purchasing - when we make the journey of 'going to the shops'.

If we disregard everyday essentials, the modern experience of shopping is one of choice, undertaken for pleasure and leisure. Audiences treat it as escapism, and look for something new to spark inspiration, for an experience with value and one that is removed from the everyday.

In a crowded marketplace, the shopkeeper must invest in techniques that enable differentiation, allowing them to stand out in the crowd and creating a draw to their offering. A unique narrative, communicated quickly and compellingly, will offer enough hooks to intrigue the audience into exploring further.

Such compelling propositions succeed in large part through creative expression and execution, and through the thoughtful detail of the presentation. If that presentation can entice audiences to dwell for longer, the chance of purchase and memorability is greater.

If the premise of the retail environment is to sell ideas, inspiration and emotive stimulation, the provision of that experience must be in keeping with that. The more successful instances visibly demonstrate the dedication of the shopkeeper to their own ideas and inspiration, and their belief in and passion for the proposition. All is driven, both consciously and subconsciously, by visual communication. In short, setting a compelling visual scene can speak silent volumes.

The shopkeeper, then, becomes not just a curator and a facilitator of transactions - a conduit to the satisfaction of good purchases - but also a stage manager and a theatre director of sorts. They must orchestrate day-to-day interaction and logistics, while also maintaining a visionary perspective and a creative, imaginative viewpoint to enable their proposition to steer a clear path, one that differs from those around it.

In a literal sense, the 'retail stage' is about setting a scene and telling a visual story, since, as we have seen, visual imagery unarguably punches more strongly than words. However, unlike a traditional theatrical stage, the notion of the retail stage invites the audience to enter and actively explore the world that has been created - to step through the 'fourth wall', the invisible barrier between the audience and the action on the stage - to interact

with it, and to buy into the vision that is being curated and presented.

On a practical level, the visual context of the products can make them more accessible, understandable, desirable and appealing, and can give them greater meaning. The setting can explain the shopkeeper's own inspiration, the origins of the product or the process of making or using it. It can build a narrative around the potential of that product's use or the benefits of its presence.

Setting an aspirational scene helps the customer to imagine how a particular product or object might fit into their life, or inspires them with suggestions about how they might enhance their own surroundings. This scene-setting approach can elevate the product and increase the perception of its value and desirability, stimulating the customer to buy a piece of the narrative to take away and create their own version.

Another argument for a visually led, immersive retail experience is that today's audiences are less enamoured than their predecessors of face-to-face service while shopping. This is not always the case, and there are scenarios in which a personal service experience is effective and welcomed (see particularly chapters Four and Nine). However, in an era of strong self-expression, in many cases audiences want to be independent, to explore and fend for themselves, to make up their own minds with no pressure to justify their decisions. Then, the visual scene in which options are presented becomes even more influential and vital as a means for the shopkeeper to express insight and perspective. If the spoken-word element is removed, customers respond favourably to the provision of plenty of visual signals, messages and explanations.

Developing a proposition around the 'retail stage' can involve a simple or opulent approach, whereby the shopkeeper either creates a context in practical terms or takes a more imaginative and fiction-

led route. It can also benefit the popular contemporary notion of the shop as a multi-use venue: a place not only for selling but also for hosting events, classes and other knowledge- and experience-based activities that enhance the business, inspire and nurture the audience and build a community around the brand. In this situation, the concept of the theatre stage as a flexible space that can be reset easily between scenes is again relevant inspiration for the shopkeeper.

Ultimately, the technique of setting the stage for retail draws on many of the strands that are covered elsewhere in this book, and it takes a creative, multi-skilled, entrepreneurial shopkeeper to steer the tone of this scene-setting to best effect. But, since audiences respond well to retail concepts that offer this immersive experience, the positive impact of investing in such an approach is as clear as the execution itself.

For years, as she scoured Europe's flea markets for treasures to populate her clients' photoshoots, the stylist, photographer and author Kara Rosenlund dreamed of one day opening a shop through which she could share her prized discoveries. But it would have to allow her to tour her wares far and wide. Now, having finally added retailer to her list of expertise, she is just as likely to be found selling her sought-after vintage treasures at markets across the Brisbane area as in the photography studio.

In celebrated 'vagabond' style, her shop, Travelling Wares, is a beautifully and lovingly restored Franklin caravan from 1956, affectionately called Frankie. The van has found fame in its own right, and is frequently spotted on highways around the region. It acts as a self-contained set, within which Rosenlund presents her wares to perfection, incorporating compact kitchen, living and bedroom scenes and giving plenty of inspiration for her many visitors to use in their own homes.

On location, following the style of the flea markets she frequents worldwide, she opens up the caravan and allows her wares to spill out over simple trestle tables and on the ground, styled irresistibly with her keen eye for little personal touches.

She focuses on seeking out original utilitarian pieces that were built to last - combining them more recently with her own design collections, such as soaps, cushions, bags and accessories - and complements the pieces on display with handwritten notes and labels that offer style advice and ideas on how best to use the items at home.

'Having a permanent shop didn't interest me; the whole allure was the travel aspect. The caravan works well because there is something so charming and nostalgic about it. People always tell me about their childhood adventures in their parents' caravans, and they want to poke around and see inside.'
- Kara Rosenlund

Address
Various locations, Brisbane, Australia
Website
www.kararosenlund.com
Founder
Kara Rosenlund

Every detail is considered, but not overdone; everything has its place and feels precious in its selection and presentation.

TIPS

. . . .

TIP 1 - Group your products into vignettes, combined with found objects and furniture, to create a textured, inspiring setting in which your customers want to spend time.

. . . .

TIP 2 - Give away ideas and style inspiration freely, with written tags on your products and suggested style tips for how to display them at home. What you give, you receive.

The informal displays encourage visitors to touch and covet the objects without worrying about disturbing a perfect presentation.

DARKROOM
LONDON, UK
...

Launched at the London Design Festival 2016, and open for just four months, this floating pop-up shop was curated by the online design store Darkroom for the interiors lifestyle brand Bert & May, to present a new collaborative range of tiles and fabrics.

Having recently decided to close their permanent shop in favour of a combination of online retailing and flexible, temporary retail collaborations, it was important to the Darkroom team that this pop-up project should feel particularly special, as the relaunch of the brand's retail presence. Its founder and designer, Rhonda Drakeford, wanted to design and launch a new collection of products specially for the unique environment, so the concept became about building a 'new world'.

The shop was housed in a traditional barge moored outside the Bert & May studio. Inside, each room was turned into a set complete with a styled selection of specially designed products for purchase. This is a distinctive Darkroom trait; the shop displays have always been as important as the products themselves, based on creative groupings and resembling artistic still-life settings.

The main feature was the installation of the Split Shift tile series, created

for Bert & May. The rear deck was clad in the monochrome and the bathroom in the blue colourway, a site-specific display method that the designers quickly realized customers found more engaging than traditional displays. Throughout the space, the Darkroom team presented the product collections using their distinctive modular display plinths in varying dimensions - on this occasion using colours from the Bert & May paint collection - set against their trademark black walls.

'It's really nice to be able to display our products in a semi-residential space, and people are always excited to see the bathroom in particular. We found it very useful to be able to show the tiles in a domestic context rather than simply in a shop window, as we had originally planned.'
- Rhonda Drakeford

Website
www.darkroomlondon.com
Founders
Rhonda Drakeford (Darkroom)
and Lee Thornley (Bert & May)

The design products were shown in the context for which they are intended, whether that be the bedroom or the shower.

TIPS

. . . .

TIP 1 - Create a full home scene for your offering within a defined space to enable your customers to see the products as they would be in their intended setting.

. . . .

TIP 2 - Context helps your customer to visualize and increases their confidence that they will make the right choice, while experiencing a complete scene builds their desire to buy into the style on show.

. . . .

TIP 3 - Keep the cash desk low-profile, to maximize the atmosphere of your immersive setting; if possible, have no cash desk at all and offer a flexible transaction process.

The shop, housed in a canal boat, quickly built up great word of mouth for its unusual setting, novel approach to retail and beautiful, creative fit-out.

The celebrated Czech paper products company Papelote began life as the graduate dissertation of one of its founders, the graphic designer and illustrator Kateřina Šachová. It now exists with a mission to breathe fresh air into the world of stationery - emphasizing beautiful aesthetics and high-quality craftsmanship, eco-friendly materials and local production, and celebrating a material that is 'full of flavour, fragrance, sound and colour' and has a long, rich history.

Soon after establishing the brand as an online business, the founders decided to open a shop so that their customers could explore the sensory world of the products. The space would serve simultaneously as showroom, shop and occasional exhibition and educational space, and would also house the team's workshop, where the majority of the products are made.

As befits the medium of the products, the ordered, playful space is pleasingly tactile, with a sense of old times. Exceptional attention to detail is shown in such features as an effective display wall that is simply a multitude of metal bulldog clips screwed directly into the plaster; a traditional school blackboard and vintage pieces linked to paper storage, such as an old plan chest; and an arched, backlit paper ceiling that brings a warm glow to the space. The bespoke merchandizing units in the centre of the floor, including the cash desk, are on wheels, so that the floor plan can be quickly and efficiently reconfigured for workshops, seminars and craft days.

'None of us had any experience with retail before we started. We have learned and are still learning on the go. What gives us most pleasure is to see the diversity of the people who come to visit our shop, and their joy in our products. That makes it all worthwhile.'
- Kateřina Šachová

Address
Vojtěšská 9, Prague 1, 110 00, Czech Republic
Website
www.papelote.eu
Founders
Kateřina Šachová, Denisa Havrdová and Filip Šach
Designer
A1 Architects (www.a1architects.cz)

TIPS

. . . .

TIP 1 - If you want a flexible
space for a variety of uses,
keep your fixtures simple and
on wheels as much as possible.
Think carefully about the
footprint before you fill
too much of the floor.

. . . .

TIP 2 - Treat the floor as a canvas
on which to build and rearrange
temporarily. Don't set rules, other
than specifying modular, easily
transformable units.

This super-simple display
solution of bulldog clips
screwed into the wall is fun
and light-hearted, and saves
on shelf space.

Display furniture in the
shop has been custom-made
and set on wheels, so it can
be easily moved around to
reconfigure the space for
classes and events.

Storage in this small space
is kept to a minimum, with a
limited number of shelves and a
vintage plan chest as a feature.

DE BALKONIE
AMSTERDAM,
THE NETHERLANDS
...

In a city of apartments opening on to canals and bustling streets, De Balkonie is a one-stop shop dedicated to helping owners decorate the many balconies that currently sit empty across the city. Recognizing that about 70 per cent of the houses in Amsterdam have a small balcony, but that most of those are neglected and left as a playground for pigeons, its founders, Friederike Joppen and Thijs Box, set about building a business that provides all the inspiration, products and advice people need to create their own private, happy spot of urban green.

Illustrating their vision and promise, the shop is packed with a wide assortment of plants, equipment, furniture and clever suggestions for maximizing small urban green spaces. The lush, vibrant space brings the concept to life through detailed scene-setting and carefully styled vignettes.

The decor of the shop is deliberately casual, using natural tones of grey and sand as a backdrop to ensure that the greenery is brought to the fore throughout. A simple podium made of wooden pallets in front of two alcoves offers a stage for changing seasonal scenes that put the furniture and plants in the context of different balcony settings. Display islands in the middle of the shop, also made from simple pallets, showcase the various plant promotions, while copper-green vintage shelving units display accessories. On fine days, these displays spill out on to the street, taking the green back out into the city.

The brand's striking visual identity revolves around bespoke pen illustrations of plants by Peter-Paul Rauwerda, a friend of the owners. These are used for the logo, across all communications and online.

'Most people don't know what they can do with their small outside spaces in the city. With some small changes, you can turn your balcony into your own little paradise. That is our mission, to provide all the tools and advice to enable people do that.'
- Thijs Box

Address
Jan Evertsenstraat 90,
1056 EG Amsterdam, The Netherlands
Website
www.debalkonie.nl
Founders
Friederike Joppen and Thijs Box
Designer
Studio Mokum (www.studiomokum.com)
Illustrator
Peter-Paul Rauwerda (www.pprauwerda.nl)

The shop is laid out clearly, with vignettes on the left and step-by-step product displays on the right as the customer enters.

TIPS
· · · · · · ·

TIP 1 - Create scenes that give
your products context and provide
visual ideas, tips and advice for
your customers.
· · · · · · ·

TIP 2 - Think about height
within your space. Where you can,
add visual interest by hanging
products, signage or decorative
elements from the ceiling,
as with a theatre set.
· · · · · · ·

TIP 3 - Take the inside out.
If your location allows, let
your products spill out on
to the street, to create an
enviable scene and invite
in passing customers.

A simple wooden podium made
of pallets presents changing
seasonal scenes that place
the furniture and products
in context.

ANDREAS MURKUDIS
BERLIN, GERMANY
...

Andreas Murkudis has worked in the art world for nearly two decades, directing the Museum der Dinge (Museum of Things) in Berlin, among other roles. When he opened his first shop - now one of five - he envisioned a place filled with objects that are dear to him and that he wanted to share with others. His vision has always been to provide a product range without limitations - to create a broad landscape of goods and ideas, both from established labels and from those that are unknown at the time of his discovery. His audience is similarly broad, from his affluent, design-conscious regular clientele to appreciative fashion students who come in to soak up inspiration and inspect the cut of a garment by a designer they particularly admire.

Murkudis considers it his mission to accumulate things of exceptional beauty and give them space to breathe. To that end, his shop is a large, airy space where he translates the idea of the 'landscape' into a topographical map of islands, presenting a variety of surfaces and platforms scattered across the floor. These flexible display features, many of which are low-level, allow a clear, uncluttered and peaceful view across the space, and present all the goods on a neutral ground, with no hierarchy and regardless of their label or price. The tableaux focus on quality, artisanship, idea and authenticity, and Murkudis is careful to allow every piece to shine in its own spotlight. His experience of working as a museum curator is pleasingly evident in this concept, resulting in an unusual, confident and respectful approach to displaying products.

'I very much enjoy talking to our customers, some of whom are long-time clients; others are real friends and some are new. I try to get to know them all and tell the stories of the products. It's all part of presenting the poetry of the shop.'
- Andreas Murkudis

Address
Potsdamerstraße 81E, 10785 Berlin, Germany
Website
www.andreasmurkudis.com
Founder
Andreas Murkudis
Designer
Gonzalez-Haase AAS (www.gonzalezhaase.com)

TIPS
. . . .

TIP 1 - Even in a big space, product displays benefit from a close connection that focuses the eye and creates complementary relationships among the pieces on display.

. . . .

TIP 2 - Experiment with creating display islands on different levels to make a landscape within which each of your selected products has its own careful positioning and focus.

Individual products are presented carefully across a landscaped island of levels, so that each has its own space and focus.

Products across a range of price points and themes are displayed alongside one another as a single interesting collection.

JOYA STUDIO
BROOKLYN, USA
...

The first flagship retail space for the artisan fragrance house Joya is presented as an 'industrial scent studio'. Part gallery and part shop, it also houses the company's full manufacturing facility.

Traditionally, fragrance houses are very secretive about their operations. The Joya team is deliberately doing the exact opposite, fostering an ethos of complete transparency and expressing the desire to allow visitors into their world, so that they too may experience the entire manufacturing process.

Joya sources rare raw materials and employs local artisans to fuse ancient manufacturing techniques with modern ingredients and technology. This clash of old and new, and the desire to reveal the production process, has strongly influenced the style of the shop, in which a raw industrial structure is contrasted with the intangible experience of fragrance.

The area at the front of the multi-use venue gives the impression of a theatre set, hung with steel and oak-veneer flats. These vertical panels are arranged to allow glimpses into the production area beyond, where the team diffuses and blends fragrances, produces candles and soaps, casts porcelain and ceramic prototypes for the fragrance bottles, and makes silicon moulds.

The panels feature spotlit display alcoves, creating a gallery feel that highlights the rarified, *objet d'art* quality of the collection of products. They slide on rails, so they can be repositioned easily to set up different views and scenes, and to create backdrops for the studio's programme of events.

'I'm really happy to show what we do, to reveal where the magic happens. I like the way it feels as if we were busy working here, and the gallery element just landed in the middle of it all.'
- Frederick Bouchardy

Address
19 Vanderbilt Avenue, Brooklyn, NY 11205, USA
Website
www.joyastudio.com
Founder
Frederick Bouchardy
Designer
Taylor & Miller (www.taylorandmiller.com)

Creating a similar experience to that of a black-box theatre, the flexible wall system used in the space enables the venue to be adapted for different types of events.

TIPS

· · · · · · ·

TIP 1 - If you make your own products on-site, but need to keep the process contained, try introducing a view in the style of a stage set to allow glimpses across the space.

· · · · · · ·

TIP 2 - Warm, targeted spotlighting on specific products demonstrates that you care about the detail, giving the product a respectful uplift and enhancing the impact of your displays.

· · · · · · ·

TIP 3 - Flexible scenery allows your space to become more than a shop, enabling you to build a community through events and to put your space on the map in a different way.

Spotlit alcoves built in to the flexible walls create the impression of an art gallery and celebrate the quality of the finely crafted products on display.

HIGHLIGHTS & LOWLIGHTS
...

APPROACH THE LIGHTING OF YOUR
PRODUCTS AND SHOP ENVIRONMENT IN
A WAY THAT CREATES ATMOSPHERE
AND FOCUSES ATTENTION WHERE
YOU WANT IT.
...

'Life is all about lighting.'
- Stevie Nicks (b. 1948)

Never underestimate the power of good lighting. As Stevie Nicks says, lighting influences all our encounters, both physical and sensory, and can affect our physiology both positively and negatively. Lighting differentiates us, defines our characteristics and explains or enhances - or can just as equally numb - the world around us. Environmentally, it articulates space, marking out boundaries, open spaces, physical features, highlights and textures of a landscape.

Whether it is used to warm up or cool down an atmosphere, to focus the attention or mellow the mind, lighting has the ability to affect our behaviour in ways that no other visual medium can. Being aware of and recognizing this is valuable when shaping a compelling narrative experience. Ignore its importance, or get it wrong, and the negative impact on the audience can be significant.

Lighting must be considered with the amount of care that is given to any other applied creative tool, since in essence it is a vital channel of daily communication. It should be used in precisely this way in the shop space, too - as a valuable communication medium, in terms of both practical and sensory activation.

Lighting sets the pace and style of any encounter. At a physical level, if specific light sources and styles are placed correctly, it is possible to influence a potential customer's journey through a space, and encourage particular interactions and responses.

In sensory terms, to be effective a retail environment must offer an experience that goes beyond purely facilitating the exchange of goods, whether it takes the form of a direct visual narrative or a more emotive, subconscious one. As in public buildings or domestic interiors, lighting can also have a strong effect on an audience's mood and receptiveness in a shop - from their perception of the value and quality of the products on offer, to their

feeling of desire to engage with or buy into the overall narrative proposition.

Just as the shopkeeper should consider the details of physical display, navigation, knowledge sharing, service and so on, so it is important to define a considered approach to the role of lighting in the experience. The results cannot be underestimated.

Light is the medium through which we are able to view our world, and therefore the most important facilitator for many other mediums of communication. If 80 per cent of the information our brains receive is channelled through our eyes, then, at an animal level, we rely both consciously and subconsciously on the quality of light in our environment to inform our decisions and behaviour and therefore our mood. Light is vital if we are to understand the world around us. The other senses also play an important role in our experiences, of course, but because of our crucial relationship with light, our responses to it in all its forms are deeply rooted.

When we consider the lighting of an environment or space we are responding to this basic element of human behaviour. Through it we must generate a certain level of comfort, security and direction. Beyond that, light can be used to set a tone, nurture a mood, generate specific emotional responses and, through that, encourage certain actions.

There is much more to the application of lighting than simply ensuring there is enough for the space to be usable. There are decisions to be made about warmth or coolness; colour, intensity and style; brightness, shading and diffusion; whether the source should be visible or hidden; and whether a fixture should be a visual feature in itself.

It should also be noted that choosing to limit sources of lighting is just as important as introducing them when we are attempting to craft an appropriate, desirable and effective atmosphere. The final lighting in your space must ensure

ease of physical activity while enhancing the psychological impression.

While low-lit environments naturally generate a stronger emotive atmosphere, and can be combined with highlights to focus the attention where it is required, brighter lighting creates more textured environments for propositions that require the communication of practical information. So, although too little light might slow activity down, too much of it can leave audiences feeling exposed and under pressure or undue stress, and that quickly has a detrimental effect.

The psychology of lighting is complex, and lighting design as a profession is highly skilled and scientific. But much is intuitive, and there are many simple techniques that the entrepreneurial shopkeeper can apply to devise a scheme that represents their proposition better than the shop-fit solutions that are offered as standard. In today's industry of choice, innovation and flexibility,

there is no excuse for bad lighting,
and no reason why it should occur.

Ultimately, lighting influences how
an audience feels - their receptiveness
to the level of energy or tranquillity in
the shop -, and whether their impression of
the proposition sparks them to action. So,
alongside the range of applied creative
disciplines explored in this book, lighting
must be embraced as part of the shopkeeper's
creative toolkit that sits at the heart of
developing a compelling and complete shop
concept and experience.

The ethical brand Marie-Stella-Maris, founded by Patrick Munsters and Carel Neuberg, sells natural care and scent products for skin, body, hair and home, alongside a symbolic assortment of mineral waters. Encouraging their audience to 'care for water', the foundershave created a brand that clearly demonstrates their belief that everyone should have access to clean drinking water. The business supports this belief through making donations to drinking-water projects worldwide, based on sales. All products are manufactured by the brand; for anything that nature cannot provide, the team searches for the safest and most responsible alternative.

The boutique space centres on a distinctive, high-impact light-box wall, with clear, cinema-style lettering that communicates concisely the company's purpose and its dedication to its belief. This visually arresting effect also ensures that the focus is on the products and the purpose, rather than on any additional creative distractions of branding or styling. The light-box wall also, of course, provides appealing ambient light across the space, lifting any shadows during the day and ensuring a compelling glow through the windows after dark. The bright, open style of the windows allows the typographic narrative to be viewed clearly by passers-by, especially outside opening hours, while the fuss-free typography is continued on the façade signage and pavement signboard.

At the back of the simply furnished shop is a large portrait taken by the Dutch art photographer Linelle Deunk on a visit to one of the clean-water projects supported by the company in Uganda. Clean, monochrome imagery is also displayed in the windows to complement rather than compete with the strong graphic interior.

'We wanted to create a clean, friendly, graphic space to communicate our message clearly and professionally, and inspire more people to contribute. We needed to make a strong but appealing statement.'
- Patrick Munsters

Address
Keizersgracht 357, 1016 EJ Amsterdam,
The Netherlands
Website
www.marie-stella-maris.com
Founders
Patrick Munsters and Carel Neuberg

The large window communicates the narrative of the products on display, particularly outside shop opening hours.

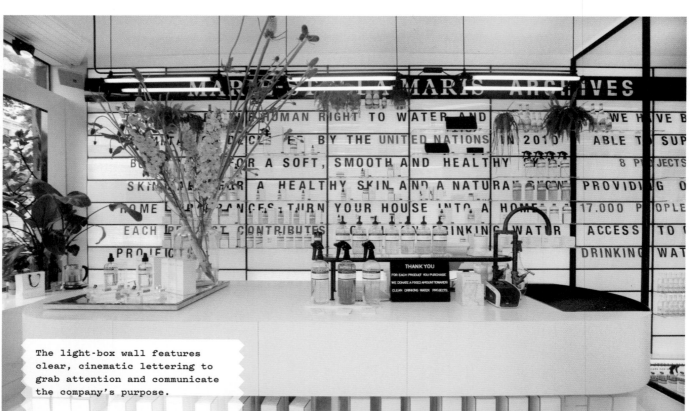

The light-box wall features clear, cinematic lettering to grab attention and communicate the company's purpose.

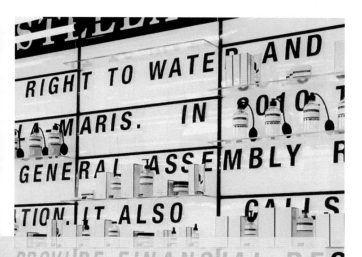

TIPS

· · · · · · ·

TIP 1 - Set aside glossy printed graphics and experiment with characterful, vibrant signage styles borrowed from other sectors, such as hospitality or entertainment.

· · · · · · ·

TIP 2 - Integrating the display walls with their own light source can bring a warm, energizing, welcoming ambience and creates compelling night-time visibility for the shop.

· · · · · · ·

TIP 3 - If a strong visual message is displayed inside your shop, don't clutter or confuse the view from outside. Daylight is precious, so keep your windows crisp, clean and bright.

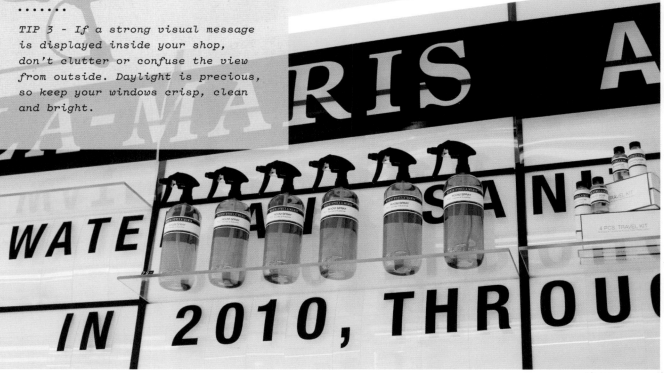

After years working in the corporate world, Monika Zagajska and Michał Jeger saw an opportunity to open an artisanal perfume laboratory - the first retail offering of its kind in Poland - where anyone can come to make their own custom fragrance. They present it as a 'magical' space with a hint of nostalgia inspired by the style of pre-war pharmacies.

As a start-up business, Zagajska and Jeger had to be resourceful and invest wisely in just a few key features, so they opted for a small, cosy, minimalist set-up revolving around a heavy central table, where the perfumes are mixed. As the business has developed, the style of these furnishings has gradually evolved, but it retains its original ethos.

The focal point of the table is enhanced by a bright, focused pool of light provided by a series of low-hanging industrial lamps along the length of the table. The process of creating a fragrance can take a few hours, so the owners recognize that it is important that the customer should feel nurtured and comfortable during that time. They have created a very special experience in which the perfumers gather with the customers on stools around the table.

Additional warm ambient lighting radiates from hidden fixtures along the back of the shelving on the product wall, illuminating the long lines of vintage pharmacy bottles holding the individual aromatic compositions, bases and scents, each clearly labelled. This backlighting technique also has the benefit of creating a halo around each bottle, elevating its presence on the shelf and allowing its contents to glow within the amber glass, contrasting with the pale labels.

'It's a great feeling to know that people like to spend a lot of time with us in our perfumery because of the atmosphere. We wanted to create an interior that enhances the work of our perfumers, that creates a mood that helps them to work the "magic" of scent creation.'
- Monika Zagajska

Address
Ul. Mokotowska 61, 00-542 Warsaw, Poland
Website
www.mo61.pl
Founders
Monika Zagajska and Michał Jeger
Designer
Buck.Studio (www.buck.pl)

TIPS
. . . .

TIP 1 - If your retail offering revolves around an expert consultancy service, consider giving that the central weighting in your space, rather than hiding it away at the back.

. . . .

TIP 2 - Backlighting products on the shelf brings out the colour and variety in the range, and gives them a glowing vibrancy that increases their presence and perceived value.

. . . .

*TIP 3 - Varying pools of warm light create a relaxed atmosphere and **make** a space more inviting for **spending** time in than uniform lights that cast a constant level of bright light.*

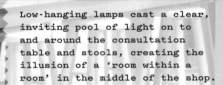

Low-hanging lamps cast a clear, inviting pool of light on to and around the consultation table and stools, creating the illusion of a 'room within a room' in the middle of the shop.

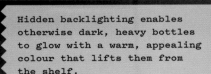

Hidden backlighting enables otherwise dark, heavy bottles to glow with a warm, appealing colour that lifts them from the shelf.

HAUS OF AYALA
PARIS, FRANCE
...

The Mexican designer Jorge Ayala, who trained in architecture, founded his eponymous fashion label as part of an exploration into how we experience visual pattern and abstract form, and the crossover between the natural world and the digital realm. Soon after he started producing catwalk collections, he realized the need to capture the inspirations of his label in a physical space, where his customers could experience the eclectic range of ideas and experiments that he weaves together. He then focused on applying to three-dimensional space the same artistic direction that he gives to fashion.

Ayala has since opened a number of boutique spaces, all embedded with the same creative flair and sophistication; they are immersive and otherworldly spaces that bring his experiments and digital concepts to life. His background in architecture leads him to push the expectations of how a space might be used, playing with perspective, texture and the boundary between virtual and physical sensation. In his latest space, his signature wallpaper adorns not just the walls but also the ceiling, while his experimental sculptures are interspersed with selected fashion pieces hung around the walls.

The light is deliberately low throughout, and the patterned walls are punctuated with handmade sculptural lighting pieces, carefully positioned to lead the eye through the space. The overall sensation is of being enveloped in Ayala's dreamworld, and lighting is used to enhance this effect. Even the practical element of lighting is given an experimental edge. He talks often about setting a scene against which mannequins can play, and every detail has been envisioned and made by him personally.

'I don't want people to see a retail space; I prefer to think of it as a curatorial space that allows people to escape, within different scenarios. My lighting style helps me create these scenarios, as you would on a stage set, and adds to the spatial experience.'
- Jorge Ayala

Address
Rue du Roi de Sicile 128, 75004 Paris, France
Website
www.ayalaparis.com
Founder
Jorge Ayala

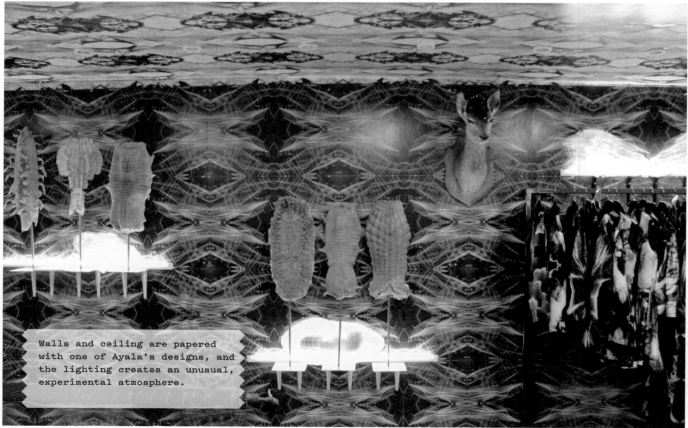

Walls and ceiling are papered with one of Ayala's designs, and the lighting creates an unusual, experimental atmosphere.

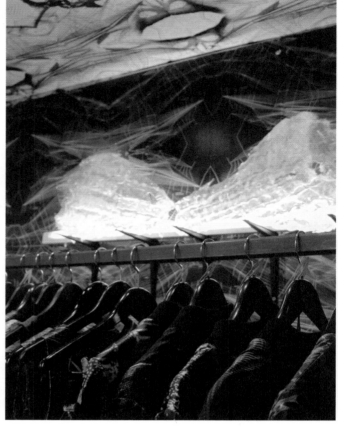

TIPS

· · · · · · ·

TIP 1 - If your brand has a strong narrative and theatrical character, explore how your shop experience might improve if it took on some of the immersive, sensory elements of a stage set.

· · · · · · ·

TIP 2 - Your shop needs lighting, but that doesn't have to be traditional retail-style. Get creative, or consider sourcing pieces that help you to create your own piece of theatre.

· · · · · · ·

TIP 3 - Your shop is a three-dimensional space, and every surface is there to be used. Don't forget that you can include the floor and ceiling in your narrative, too.

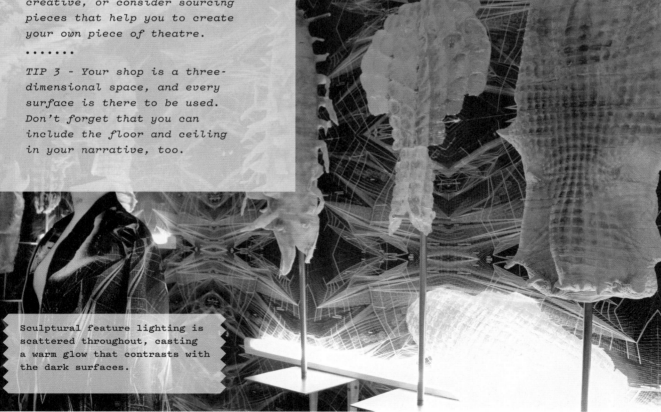

Sculptural feature lighting is scattered throughout, casting a warm glow that contrasts with the dark surfaces.

STORYTAILORS
LISBON, PORTUGAL
...

For four years the celebrated Portuguese couture designers Luis Sanchez and João Branco worked behind closed doors in an atelier, receiving their clients by appointment only. In 2007 they opened a shop in a stripped-back historic warehouse in the heart of old Lisbon, treating it as a transformable stage set in which they could welcome and, notably, entertain their customers. Spread across two floors, and integrating alcoves and charming historic features, the versatile venue allows the two men to tell an evolving and eclectic story to match their imaginative, multi-dimensional fashion creations, to translate the Storytailors concept and vision - previously developed in print and online - into an immersive sensory showcase. Lighting plays a key role in setting the scene and ambience, and combines a range of juxtaposed styles and purposes, creating an experience that is more akin to the theatre than to a traditional shop. Soft, warm pools of light on the walls bring out the texture of the old stone and backlight the rails of garments. Overhead spotlights pick out individual garments, while striking chandeliers create a celebratory atmosphere and add a nostalgic element found in old couture houses.

Meanwhile, on the mezzanine where the designers now have their atelier, they frequently set up photoshoots for their creations, using the textures and details of the building as a backdrop and setting up contrasting studio lighting. The inspiration for the garments and shoots is often tragic fictional or historical characters, so this set-up and the resulting photographs build further on the theatrical atmosphere of the venue.

'We looked for a space with a story and an identity that would merge with ours. Then we stripped it down to its essence and implemented simple, versatile elements that would allow change and transformation, just like the design details in our garments.'
- João Branco

Address
Calçada do Ferragial 8,
1200-184 Lisbon, Portugal
Website
www.storytailors.pt
Founders
Luis Sanchez and João Branco

195

Studio lighting is introduced for couture photoshoots, bringing theatricality and glamour to the ambience.

TIPS
·······
TIP 1 - People talk about 'retail theatre', but it is rarely manifested literally. Your brand has a story to tell, and your shop is your valuable stage, so don't hold back.
·······
TIP 2 - Explore the effect of lowering the overall lighting level in your shop, keeping brighter, focused accents. See how it brings out a different quality in your products.
·······
TIP 3 - Mix it up: use varied styles of lighting in different parts of your shop, for multiple purposes or to create different atmospheres. But do have a plan, or it risks becoming cluttered.

The space has been treated as a stage set and features eclectic lighting styles that draw attention to the distinctive character of the garments on display.

Paper & Tea's mission is to encourage greater awareness and appreciation of the benefits of enjoying high-quality artisanal tea. Its founder, Jens de Gruyter, who inherited a passion for tea from his tea-trader godfather, wanted to create a retail offering that was inspired by his experiences of the rituals of tea-drinking in China, Taiwan and Japan. However, since this approach to tea was more purist than the traditional habits of tea-drinking in the West, he was aware that the shop would need to communicate in a different way.

De Gruyter deliberately turned away from the conventional over-the-counter etiquette of apothecary-style tea shops, and looked instead at how sophisticated fashion or cosmetics are presented. The result is a fusion of traditional Asian influences, such as paper screens, lanterns and origami, with modern urban touches such as the scripted lighting features. This serene environment creates the backdrop not just for product displays but also for regular tea-tasting sessions, workshops and seminars.

The precision of the tea-drinking ritual is echoed in the details of the visual communications and presentation around the space. The style of the refined, scripted neon feature lighting reflects this precision. It is used both to create aesthetic atmosphere and as a way to communicate, since the eye is naturally drawn to highlights. It clearly defines and focuses attention on the different steps in the tea-making process, and helps customers to navigate the different components of the proposition.

'I wanted the store to be a place of wonder, for people to be rewarded with the same feelings I had when I had my moments of epiphany discovering good, real tea. The way the retail system works is key to this, so customers can use all their senses to discover and learn.'
- Jens de Gruyter

Address
Alte Schönhauserstraße 50, 10623 Berlin-Mitte, Germany
Website
www.paperandtea.com
Founder
Jens de Gruyter
Designers
Fabian von Ferrari (www.fabianvonferrari.com)
with Jens de Gruyter

Brewing Serving Storage Water

TIPS

. . . .

TIP 1 - Lighting as a communication medium is ubiquitous on the street, but less so indoors. It is a simple and effective way to focus the eye and aid navigation.

. . . .

TIP 2 - Display islands can be a welcoming way to encourage dwell time, making your space feel more cosy, especially when combined with overhead pools of light.

. . . .

TIP 3 - Rather than sticking to the standard white, experiment with feature walls in stronger colours to break up a large space into 'rooms' and help to define different themes.

Neon signage catches the eye, and the sharp, handwritten style contrasts well with the natural materials of the products and display surfaces.

Pools of light from overhead spotlights make the walls glow, and bounce welcoming warm light back on to the displayed products and into the room.

A single downward spotlight highlights the demonstration table, without the need for any collateral to be made visible.

THE NEW CRAFTSMEN
LONDON, UK
...

Beginning with an online presence and two temporary shops, this celebrated promoter of contemporary British craft subsequently expanded into its current permanent space. As well as showcasing and selling the work of the finest British craft makers, the New Craftsmen's space integrates a schedule of rotating exhibitions, workshops and demonstrations, all with the aim of involving visitors in the backstory, processes, materials and skills of the nation's craft heritage.

The space is presented as a sanctuary, removed from the hustle and bustle; it is raw and airy, with plenty of natural light from the skylights. The layout encourages the customer to explore various scenes and room settings, presenting the individual craft pieces to best effect. Lighting is used effectively as a feature throughout, creating a welcoming atmosphere.

In 2016 the team curated Makers House, a temporary workshop that formed part of the luxury brand Burberry's show home. This immersive experience presented demonstrations by both established and fledgling makers, carefully selected by the New Craftsmen to bring to life the inspiration of Burberry's newest collection. Central to the format was a large work table, framed in a warm pool of light cast by low-hung industrial lamps, which encouraged visitors to gravitate towards this hub of activity. In contrast, the wider, flexible event space featured industrial studio lighting, which created a rhythm of highlights and shadows and brought a heightened, theatre-set feel to the experience.

Also in 2016, for Art Basel, the New Craftsmen team created the Nature Lab installation. Simple spotlighting contrasted with natural materials, leading the eye down to a concise display that focused attention on the textures and forms of the featured pieces.

'Our ambition is to be a true hub for buying, commissioning, learning about and making fine craft. We provide the platform and the environment that allows the makers to do what they do best - making.'
- Natalie Melton

Address
34 North Row, London W1K 6DG, UK
Website
www.thenewcraftsmen.com
Founders
Natalie Melton, Mark Henderson and Catherine Lock

The highlights and shadows falling across the floor enhance the show-like feel of the space, and direct the viewer's attention to the table.

Stage lighting adds contrast, and casts pools of light across the space, creating focal points as well as the necessary lowlights.

Low-hung industrial bulbs above the workshop table focus the eye on the colours, textures and activities on its surface.

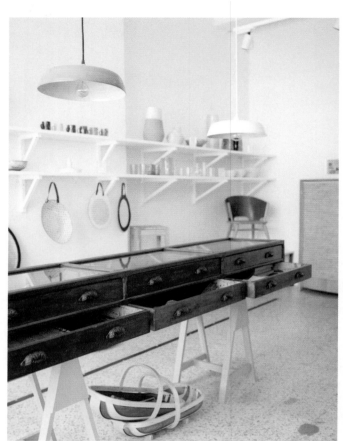

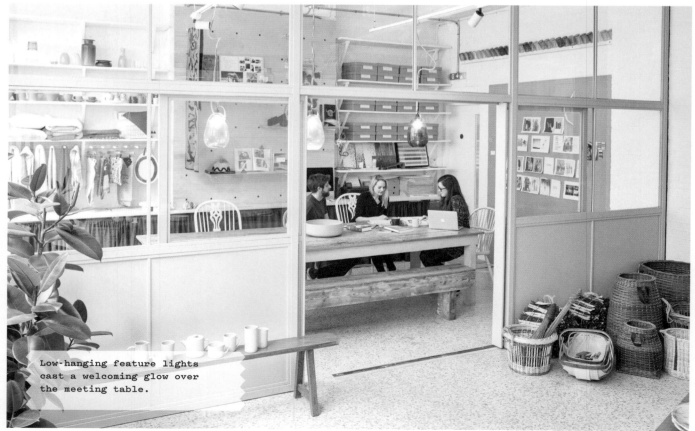

Low-hanging feature lights cast a welcoming glow over the meeting table.

TIPS

• • • • • • •

TIP 1 - Experiment with landscaping your space using a mixture of feature lighting pieces, to create various focal points, welcoming scenes and cosy corners.

• • • • • • •

TIP 2 - Overhead lighting doesn't have to be at ceiling height. Hang your lights low over tables to draw the eye and create a warm glow around a particular activity.

• • • • • • •

TIP 3 - If you host events, explore using a variety of lighting to change the mood from day to evening, and from shop to class to party.

FAÇADES & GLIMPSES
...

YOUR SHOPFRONT TELLS A VITAL STORY
ABOUT YOUR BRAND, DAY AND NIGHT,
SO MAKE THE MOST OF THIS VIEWPOINT
WITH CONFIDENT VISUAL ENGAGEMENT.
...

'The whole world of colour and of art are considered by the artistic window-dresser as his field of supply.'
- Harry Selfridge

In the Louis Vuitton archives is a copy of an article that the visionary retailer Gaston-Louis Vuitton wrote in 1925 on the subject of shop windows, for the French design magazine Vendre. In it, he celebrated the art of the window display and its ability to bring joy and visual excitement to the streets. 'Let's draw the passer-by, let's give him a reason to dawdle, to stroll!' he wrote passionately. Vuitton's statement is testament to a pioneering passion and drive to innovate and champion excellence that has inspired countless shop owners, brands and retail teams, and which set in motion the competitive movement of exceptional window displays that we admire so much across the world today.

Vuitton also wrote that those responsible for creating effective window displays required 'both a sharp sense of architecture and the skills of a stage director'. As seen throughout this book, such skills are still very relevant today in the multifaceted toolkit of the entrepreneurial shopkeeper.

Harry Selfridge, too, celebrated the prowess of the window-dresser as an artist and explorer of cultural commentary. He described eloquently how any person in that role must keep their horizons ever-expanding and open, and draw inspiration from wider cultural and artistic fields, in order to paint both relevant and aspirational pictures within the window frame that would captivate passers-by and spark them to action.

Window displays in our contemporary marketplace remain a constantly evolving exploration of communications techniques and display solutions. Arguably, they must now work harder than ever to cut through the noise of the street and the many and varied commercial messages, to differentiate an offering, build value and create a compelling case for patronizing one particular business over another.

In a marketplace that is more competitive than ever, window displays have never been more critical to the success of a physical retail proposition. The audience's attention span is much reduced from the days of Selfridge and Vuitton - the effect of a combination of too much commercial messaging, and our ability to be 'somewhere else' through digital technology while walking down the street. It is the role of the shop window to re-engage those passing audiences, to surprise, delight and captivate them and to instil in them the desire for action. It can provide the stimulation that 'trips' the passer-by out of their daydream and encourages them to break with the norm.

Such visual displays offer an opportunity for a form of textured, dynamic communication that is not found anywhere else in retail. They are a form of advertising in three dimensions, advertising at its most tangible and tactile, encouraging and facilitating the desire for immediate connections.

The windows and larger façade of a shop must work hard to encourage audiences

to cross the physical and subconscious
threshold and engage further. The most
effective displays break through the
barrier between interior and street,
reaching out visually if not physically,
so that the audience feels engaged and
involved and the threshold dissolves.

In simple terms, shop windows frame
the view into the shop, of the products
or of the activity on display. But rather
than a static medium, it is important for
the shopkeeper to consider them as a two-
way portal, through which the essence and
character of the shop are drawn out to the
world passing by and the energy of that
world is drawn in, almost as though through
a process of breathing.

Despite its glass façade, the window
display is not a two-dimensional canvas,
but a multilayered, textural space, a small
stage set. It captures a moment of theatre
or a visual story told concisely, and
entices the audience to find out more
and choose to give value to the experience.

Although it is certainly the case that
physical window displays are only ever seen
by a certain number of passers-by, it is
worth considering that the most inspired
examples are often photographed by those
onlookers and shared with their communities
and networks. The beautiful, aspirational
window display therefore has the potential
to take on a second existence as digital
content, and to find a bigger audience -
and potential future customer base - online.
That is certainly a fine incidental benefit
for any business.

Windows speak to a passing audience
twenty-four hours a day, even when the
shop is closed. They will therefore speak
negatively as well as positively, if these
out-of-hours encounters have not also been
considered by the shopkeeper. It is perhaps
particularly important to communicate
well when the shop is shut, to encourage
future visits. Practically, if the shop
has obligatory shutters at night, there
is nothing to stop the shopkeeper from

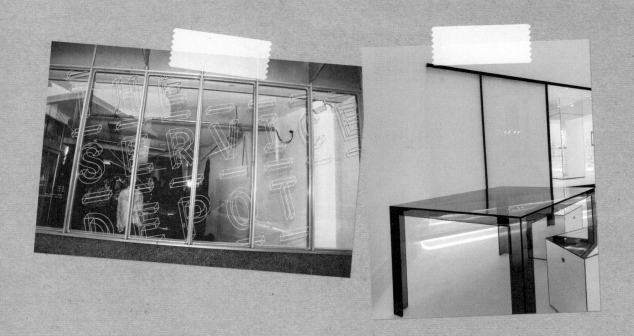

reappraising that screen as a canvas through which to communicate. Every encounter is important, and the message the shop façade portrays need not focus only on what sits behind the window frame.

Louis Vuitton closed his article by describing 'a wind of change...blowing in this new century', through which shopkeepers' windows across the city were transformed into a 'magnificent and modern façade'. With the booming entrepreneurial marketplace that is bringing exciting creativity and innovative concepts back to our shopping streets in increasing numbers, this same wind just might be blowing welcome new energy into the retail scene in ever more inspiring ways.

The classically trained English milliner Fiona Bennett opened her first shop in central Berlin in the late 1990s, with the aim of rescuing the fading art of hat-making and encouraging an appreciation of this intricate craftsmanship by bringing it into the heart of fast-paced modern city culture. In 2012 she took it a step further, joining forces with Hans Boehme to make a strong statement on shop design. This new flagship celebrates Bennett's creative and craft process and brings it out into the open, through a working studio placed in the window facing the main street. This small atelier space - in which her milliners sit at a large workbench, dressed as impeccably as the hats they are making - is an eye-catching spectacle, glowing like a stage set when it falls dark outside, as well as demonstrating the true artisan skills of the business.

Bennett and Boehme's approach to the shop revolves around the notion of presenting a 'playground for adults', in which they can introduce their customers to the complete world of Bennett's designs. While the window presentation is more akin to a moment of theatre, the shop itself takes inspiration from the simplicity of art galleries, in a simple monochromatic style with Baroque detailing. Every piece shines, and is given space to show off its own personality. Within this environment the world-renowned and often extravagant hats are presented as wearable pieces of art.

At every touchpoint, the creative energy of the making process is apparent and made central to the experience, ensuring that buying a piece of Bennett's work becomes a memorable event in itself, even before the occasion at which the hat will be worn.

'We wanted to bring back the joyfulness of the hat as an accessory. We love the open studio and the transparency of the space to the street. It is so great to observe our customers' fascination and the magical attraction of this window into our world.'
- Fiona Bennett

Address
Potsdamerstraße 81-83,
D-10785 Berlin, Germany
Website
www.fionabennett.com
Founders
Fiona Bennett and Hans Boehme

Fiona Bennett / Berlin

The mirrored back wall of the workshop reflects both the scene and the light from the street, making the window space feel larger.

The complete construction process for the hats is on show, with a simplicity and honesty that make for compelling viewing for passers-by outside.

The display of the working process has been thought through carefully, down to the sleek traditional apron uniforms.

The authentic craft of making the hats, rather than an on-demand staged show, gives the brand a friendly personality.

TIPS
. . . . . .

TIP 1 - Consider whether the
craft process behind making your
products is one that could become
a visually arresting activity for
your windows, stopping passers-by
in their tracks.

. . . .

TIP 2 - It can be more beneficial
to use your windows to *frame* a
glimpse of the *life* within your
business and shop than to close
them off with static displays
of products.

. . . .

TIP 3 - Bring a little *magic* to the
street by *framing* your windows as
if they are a stage set, where the
curtains have been drawn back to
reveal a *dynamic* scene.

This is the second international outpost of the Indonesian hospitality group Potato Head. It is a striking boutique space with a simple, flexible design that revolves around a grid system in white-painted steel, matched by white walls and floor.

The larger share of the retail space is taken by Canaan, a high-end lifestyle boutique from Bali, curated by its owner and shopkeeper, Emmelyn Gunawan, and offering textiles, accessories and homewares made by craftspeople across Indonesia. Contrasting effectively with the stark white geometric display structures, the product range is consciously anchored around a bold colour scheme of soft and deep tones, creating the visual effect of a floating formation of colour 'pops' across the space.

The remaining section of the shop is dedicated to merchandise from Potato Head's various brands, as well as offering a collection of magazines and vinyl, again scattered across the same landscaped steel grid and varying levels of display platforms. This area is combined with the ILOVEYOUSO coffee bar, and integrates one of the most striking visual features of the shop: a folding front window. This allows the full façade to be opened up - when the weather permits - so that the structural grid and eclectic product displays can spill out on to the pavement, at various heights and eye levels, breaking down the usual barrier between window-shopping and touching the products on display. The light and unobtrusive nature of the modular display structure also ensures good visibility into the café and shop beyond, reminding the passing customer that there is plenty more to discover indoors.

'My favourite time in the shop is during the day, when I really feel the ambience - when the light streams in through the large window, and you can see the texture of each textile piece.'
- Emmelyn Gunawan

Address
100 Third Street, Sai Ying Pun, Hong Kong, China
Websites
www.pttfamily.com; www.canaanbali.com
Shopkeeper
Emmelyn Gunawan (Canaan)
Designer
Sou Fujimoto (www.sou-fujimoto.net)

POTATO HEAD

The strikingly patterned
concertina shop window can
be folded back to allow the
varying levels of tactile
product displays to spill
on to the pavement outside.

TIPS

. . . .

TIP 1 - A simple, modular display structure means that you can easily and cost-effectively re-landscape your space regularly, to keep it fresh and inviting to explore.

. . . .

TIP 2 - Weather and location permitting, allow your retail offering to spill out from the doorway of your shop to soften the façade and entice passers-by to step inside.

. . . .

TIP 3 - A window display set on many levels intrigues the eye for longer and allows more products to be presented, while letting each shine out in its own space.

The product displays maximize the daylight coming in through the large windows, and plenty of interspersed greenery creates an indoor-outdoor feel.

THE SERVICE DEPOT
WELLINGTON, NEW ZEALAND
...

Having grown up with a passion for seeking out new fashion stories, Angela Gordon focused her second foray into fashion retail, The Service Depot, on a commitment to representing home-grown talent from across the booming New Zealand fashion design scene, alongside favourite discoveries from her travels overseas.

The shop is large and completely flexible, with no permanent fixtures, and Gordon views it as a creative playground or a giant, immersive dressing-up box. The versatility and minimalism of the space suit it to regular transformation for the wide range of collection launches, exhibitions, live-streamed gigs and catwalk shows that populate the busy events calendar, as well as the fashion displays themselves and installations created by invited artists. This open attitude creates an eclectic, welcoming atmosphere and a strong community of supporters, and the events programme has taken on a legendary status in the city.

Most notable visually are the huge windows, which connect the shop to the vibrant, creative city-centre street and turn the whole space into a bright and visually arresting stage set, especially in the evenings. This asset is emphasized by orientating the installations and activities towards this viewpoint. The schedule of creative displays develops organically, inspired by new designers Gordon has spotted or by artists who pitch concepts. The glass is kept completely clear, except for the large vinyl logo, which promotes the brand very effectively in the many photos that are taken and shared from outside during events.

'I like to challenge the establishment, and I'm all about having as much fun as possible while doing so. Our store is about freedom of expression and being irreverent, while sharing a love of fashion. Basically we love giant dress-ups!'
- Angela Gordon

Address
126 Wakefield Street, Wellington, New Zealand
Website
www.theservicedepot.co.nz
Founder
Angela Gordon
Designer
Ryan Henderson, Degree Design
(www.degreedesign.co.nz)

Rather than being closed off with product displays, the windows come alive at night with views of the activity inside.

TIPS

· · · · · · ·

TIP 1 - Your windows can offer a glimpse into any part of your business that you choose. Keeping them clear of product displays, and putting people in them instead, can have amazing results.

· · · · · · ·

TIP 2 - As part of the curation of your shop, look for opportunities to bring in creative collaborators to devise installations or displays that enhance and complement your style.

· · · · · · ·

TIP 3 - Encourage passers-by to snap and share images of your eye-catching window activity - but take advantage of this word of mouth by placing your branding clearly in the frame.

At night, targeted lighting above the window, shining on specific garments, turns the space into a theatre set that encourages visual engagement with the interior.

THE PLANETS ARE ALIGNED FOR YOU

IT'S WRITTEN IN THE STARS

C_29 OPTOMETRIST
ATHENS, GREECE
...

After ten years working in other optical stores, C_29's founder, Filippos Psinakis, decided to open his own shop with the philosophy of promoting good design in a peaceful, efficient atmosphere. His optical store, spread across a series of interconnecting rooms in a characterful listed building, offers high-end optometric consultancy and a range of refined eyewear for design-conscious customers. In order to bring in more natural light and expand the retail footprint, the latest 'room' to be added is a rear courtyard, which has been transformed into an outdoor showroom and event space.

This new room, which sits at the heart of the shop experience, has no ceiling or facade but is defined by a geometric frame of steel bars and black-painted lines, with a thickly painted white floor and side walls. A network of fine white strings hinting at barely perceptible walls also contributes to creating the visual illusion of a complete cube-shaped room.

The illusion is enhanced by indoor-style overhead lighting suspended from a sculptural arrangement of fine wires spanning the perimeter walls, while the courtyard is furnished with sculptural furniture and display surfaces that would more usually be expected in an indoor gallery. No products are displayed permanently here, however. Adding a surreal aspect, a real tree grows up through the floor of this newly imagined room.

'I wanted a space that I could use as a gallery, a room for artistic events and a space where clients can relax during their appointments. These experiences should always feel serene and peaceful, and bringing the indoors outside is a special thing to be able to offer.'
- Filippos Psinakis

Address
Kriezotou 5, Chalkida, Euboea Island, Greece
Founder
Filippos Psinakis
Designer
Studio 314 (www.314architecturestudio.com)

TIPS

. . . .

TIP 1 - If you have vacant outdoor space, give it new life by turning it into an outdoor room with a purpose. Every square foot can benefit your brand story.

. . . .

TIP 2 - If your shop is not a permanent space but rather a market stall or pop-up, explore how you can temporarily use the ground and surrounding walls to greater advantage.

LOCAL HEROES
EDINBURGH, SCOTLAND
...

The creative producer Dr Stacey Hunter developed the concept of Local Heroes in order to showcase and sell beautiful new design souvenirs by leading Scottish designers, as part of Scotland's Year of Innovation, Architecture and Design in 2016.

At first located in the grounds of Edinburgh Airport - and reaching an audience from an estimated 120 countries worldwide - the month-long pop-up project was open over the summer to promote some of Scotland's finest designers, and provided a unique opportunity for diverse audiences of tourists and resident travellers to appreciate and buy items that celebrate the country's contemporary design talent. The brief to the specially selected designers was to reimagine the concept of the 'souvenir', and produce a travel-themed and covetable object for sale in the pop-up and online.

The temporary, self-sufficient exhibition and retail unit behaved as a fold-out, walk-in shop window, intricately merchandized to highlight each of the featured products. The bold, colourful visual style was deliberately reminiscent of summer-holiday nostalgia, and was intended to portray a sense of optimism and celebration. Just one of each product was displayed, as in an exhibition environment, and stock for purchase was kept in a hidden, space-saving stockroom built into the left-hand side of the container, with a false wall linking through to the display.

After this initial pop-up activation, there are longer-term plans for the Local Heroes unit to tour to other cities and perhaps also internationally. Meanwhile, the pieces continue to be available directly from each of the featured designers.

'I chose a shipping container because it's a great symbol of internationalism, which is what Local Heroes is firmly rooted in. The format worked because it provided a home that was bold, robust and confident — it stopped people in their tracks and transgressed tired stereotypes.'
- Stacey Hunter

Website
www.localheroes.design
Founder
Dr Stacey Hunter
Designer
Old School Fabrications
(www.oldschoolfabrications.co.uk)
Bespoke typeface
Martin Baillie (www.martinbaillie.com)

LOCAL

LOCAL HEROES

Every surface was used
cleverly. This door displayed
catalogues of the product
collection, folding away
neatly when the shop was
unmanned at night.

HEROES

LOCAL HEROES

The whole unit acted as a shop window. One of each piece was displayed, and extra stock was hidden behind the scenery.

Every product had its own place and careful focus, and its own specially designed display method, like an exhibit in a gallery.

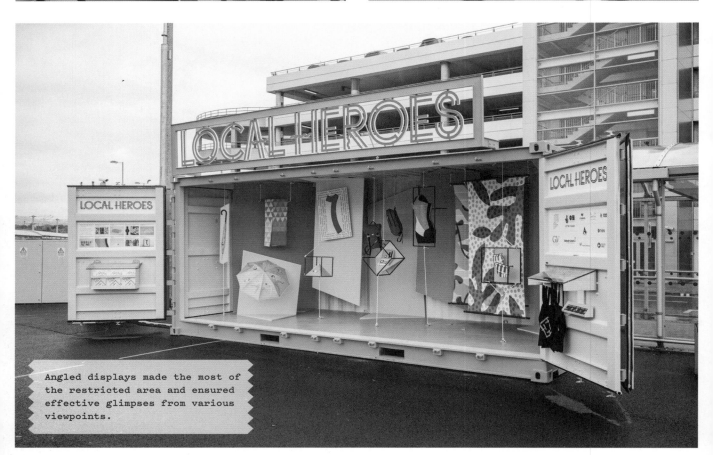

Angled displays made the most of the restricted area and ensured effective glimpses from various viewpoints.

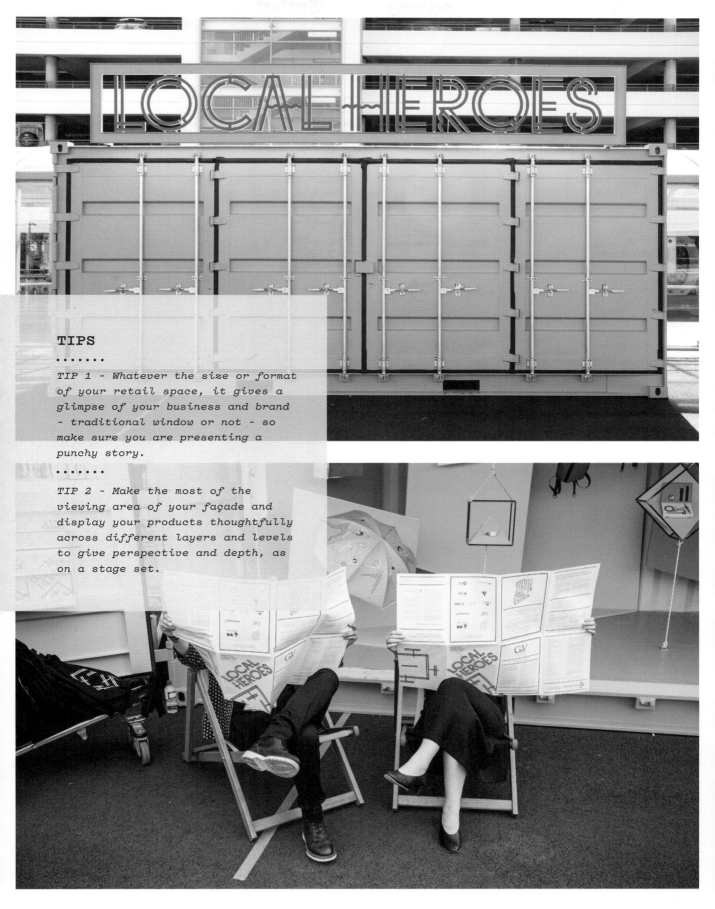

TIPS
. . . .
TIP 1 - Whatever the size or format of your retail space, it gives a glimpse of your business and brand - traditional window or not - so make sure you are presenting a punchy story.
. . . .
TIP 2 - Make the most of the viewing area of your façade and display your products thoughtfully across different layers and levels to give perspective and depth, as on a stage set.

Out of the land of fire and ice is emerging an energetic new brand that is taking the craft chocolate industry by storm. Founded by Kjartan Gíslason and Óskar Þórðarson in 2013, Omnom chocolate is winning a growing number of international awards, and reaching admiring audiences further and further across the globe.

A professional chef with expertise in pastry and baking, Gíslason was curious about the emerging craft chocolate scene. He started to experiment, and found that he had a talent - resulting in the creation of the first craft chocolate brand in Iceland.

The company began life in a tiny kitchen in a characterful old converted petrol-station kiosk. It rapidly outgrew those surroundings, however, and in 2016 it moved to new premises, a warehouse space with an impressive commercial kitchen where the complete, complex chocolate-making process is overseen carefully from bean to bar.

The team has carved out a space at the front of the warehouse floor for a shop - their first, since the previous premises was not big enough and their sales were at first only wholesale. Because there is no shop window to the street, they have introduced their own, complete with stylized awning overhead: an internal glass wall, which frames a glimpse into the active chocolate kitchen and its various machinery.

The making of chocolate is a highly skilled, scientific process that is rarely on show to customers. For this pioneering young company, which is challenging the traditions of an ancient industry, the 'window into their world' could not be better placed.

'Our shop is in our factory, so we wanted to celebrate that. We introduced a special viewing window because we want our customers to be able to see our world, who we are and how we make what we love!'
- Kjartan Gíslason

Address
Hólmaslóð 4, 101 Reykjavík, Iceland
Website
www.omnomchocolate.com
Founders
Kjartan Gíslason and Óskar Þórðarson
Devvvsign
André Úlfur Visage and Veronica Filippin

TIPS

·······

TIP 1 - If your craft business is based in a workshop with no window to the street, try making your own internal shop window to *frame* a different glimpse of your story.

·······

TIP 2 - Some products are not suited to being piled up in volume for display. If your product is *fresh* and limited-run, celebrate that with small, simple displays and big, bold graphics.

CONSIDER THE MOMENTS OF INTERACTION - THE DETAILS OF SERVICE DURING THE SHOPPING JOURNEY - THAT MAKE A POSITIVE LASTING IMPRESSION.
…

'The only thing that counts is a satisfied customer.'
- Jan Carlzon (b. 1941)

At its soul, good retail and a good shopping experience are about the people involved, whether through physical interaction or through the gestures imparted via other tools and media.

Throughout this book, we have touched on the attention to detail that is required in creating a shop environment and its many facets. The positive or negative effect of such dedication to the details or the absence of such dedication is never more apparent than in the way audiences respond to the little gestures and signals that are involved in providing efficient, expert and pleasurable service. Such signals are picked up subliminally by audiences as much as they are noted overtly, and can have a strong impact on the decision-making process and the customer's desire to engage further.

There are many elements to consider: how the shop is staffed, the atmosphere created through human encounters, the tone of voice and turn of phrase - both written and verbal - the sound and scent of the space, the way the product is packaged for taking away after purchase, and the attitude towards welcoming, nourishing and building a community around the proposition. All these elements create engaging and memorable personality, help to forge connections and build trust, and nurture belief - all of which benefit the business both immediately and in the long term.

Providing good service demonstrates the shopkeeper's dedication to and belief in the business, and their joy, pride and confidence in the product. This in turn makes the customer feel respected and appreciated, leading them to associate that experience with delight and time well spent. They will then attribute greater value to the encounter, and be more likely to patronize the shop in the future, not to mention recommending that others do the same. Excellent, authentic service is crucial in encouraging word of mouth.

The best executions of service show consideration for each of the many moments of encounter for the audience when interacting with a commercial proposition, whether before, during or after purchase. The notion of 'moments of truth' - the varied points of interaction between a customer and a proposition, that give that customer an opportunity to form an impression - as a science to be studied was developed in the 1980s by the Swedish businessman Jan Carlzon, in his book of that title. He claimed that we may encounter as many as 50,000 moments of truth every day, a fact that makes an even stronger case for the competitive execution of these moments within the retail scene in order to differentiate from and gain attention and patronage over the competition.

Service is a tool by which knowledge and expertise can be imparted in a way that is more involving, memorable and beneficial to the customer. The style, tone and attention to detail of the packaging, the labelling and the manner in which the purchase is presented for taking home, meanwhile,

add great perceived value and enhance the customer's feeling of having made a good purchase. Final crucial aspects are the sensory, unseen elements of sound and scent and the subliminal effects of a particular turn of phrase in welcoming, explaining to and thanking everyone who passes through the shop.

As with lighting, subtracting is as important here as adding. The shopkeeper should by no means include every single service element and gesture outlined here in their proposition. For example, some shop concepts benefit more than others from having background music. Some naturally associate themselves with authentic scents that add to the instinctive appeal to the customer, and these can be enhanced where appropriate; but for others this would be a distraction or an unnecessary falseness. If the chosen approach to a particular element is, in fact, to remove that element from the equation, that is perfectly acceptable. But it does pay to have considered an approach

to each, and to justify the action, since this gives focus and clarity of purpose to the final experience and that will be detected by customers.

The atmosphere created by a good service experience also helps to bring the wider business proposition or 'lifestyle' vision to life. Already in this book we have explored the visual techniques that can be applied to create immersive narrative environments. But just as important is the human element, where appropriate and if delivered in a manner that is invited by the customer and not intrusive or counter-intuitive to the flow of the experience.

It is through this human element of service that the invaluable aspect of community can be really forged and nurtured. The network that develops around an independent business is a vital life source and one that requires great dedication and investment of energy, resources and belief to build up and nourish. The hope is then that this network

will reciprocate with support, valuable
feedback and on-going patronage. It is
certainly true that happy, engaged customers
make the best ambassadors for any business.
  Because of the human focus and the
personal, emotive aspects involved in the
development of each of the gestures and
signals outlined here, it is less easy
to define a definitive output than it is
for the other practical visual tools and
techniques explored in this book. Much is
intuitive for the shopkeeper, but one thing
is certain: we must create a genuine feeling
of welcome and appreciation of the customer
at each step of the journey.

HERITAGE GENERAL STORE
CHICAGO, USA
...

Said to be Chicago's original bike café, this charming, characterful venue prides itself first and foremost on the promise of customer satisfaction - whether that's serving a great coffee or mending a puncture. Part café, part shop and part bicycle workshop, this neighbourhood space brings together the ever-popular combination of coffee and bikes, but with a highly crafted and delightfully personal touch. It's a place where customers have been known to walk in for a latte and leave with a beautiful, vintage-inspired, locally handcrafted bicycle. Almost every detail of the proposition champions the best products made in the United States - often in Chicago - from bike parts and helmets to clothing, accessories, food and coffee. The team is also proud to produce the first completely Chicago-made bicycles since Schwinn production left the city in the early 1980s.

Every part of the shop is staffed by enthusiasts and experts in cycle culture, and the founder, Mike Salvatore, might even be the one to serve you your coffee, while telling you stories from their community. Attentive, knowledgeable service is key to the success of the business, and no detail is too small - from the sharply cut aprons to the handwritten notes to the old-world jam jars in which the cold-brew coffee is served.

The community culture is strengthened by the Heritage General Store's acclaimed Heritage Cycling club, an inclusive way for new and seasoned enthusiasts to meet and ride together in the heart of Chicago, with a friendly code of conduct that promises to turn bicycle-club stereotypes on their heads.

'Our shop is not just a shop, it's an artistic space, a working space, a space to live in. We encourage everyone to bring suggestions and feedback; to bring their kids, or their laptops; and to make new friends. Everything we do is centred on this sense of community.'
- Mike Salvatore

Address
2959 N Lincoln Avenue, Chicago, IL 60657, USA
Website
www.heritagebicycles.com
Founder
Mike Salvatore

The shopkeepers take pride in every detail, down to the well-crafted branding, which is featured on the uniforms.

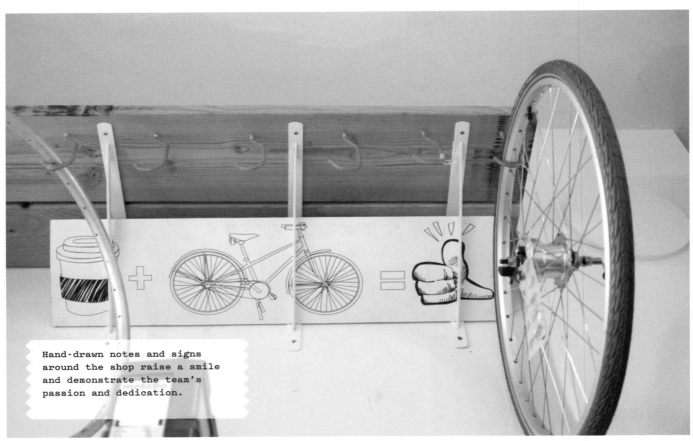

Hand-drawn notes and signs around the shop raise a smile and demonstrate the team's passion and dedication.

TIPS

· · · · · · ·

TIP 1 - The most valuable gesture you can make is one of welcome. Carve out space to encourage your audience to linger and they will help you to build that all-important sense of community.

· · · · · · ·

TIP 2 - The personal touch counts for a lot, from hand-crafted features to an 'open-plan attitude' that allows your audience to see the workings and experience the passion behind the business.

· · · · · · ·

TIP 3 - Review every 'moment of encounter' as the customer journeys through your service experience, and explore how you can make each one the best and most memorable it can be.

PÄRLANS KONFEKTYR
STOCKHOLM, SWEDEN
...

A pillar of the renowned traditional Swedish sweet-making scene, and an obligatory destination in its neighbourhood, this boutique confectioner specializes in handmade caramels and caramel sauces, all presented with perfectly executed vintage flair. Founded by Lisa Ericson, a keen Lindy hop dancer, the shop creates a highly desirable offering through deliberately resisting contemporary trends and the expectations of modern aesthetics, instead serving up a unique experience.

Every detail of the shop - the packaging and communications, the beautiful uniforms, the nostalgic jazz - transports visitors back to the 1930s, the decade in which caramels first became popular commercially, and also the era of the lively Lindy hop swing dance. Drawing on the enduring appeal of the music, fashion and design of that decade and the 1940s, every detail of the experience is carefully considered - from the hand-stamped sweet wrappers to the theatre of the hand-wrapping process, which takes place in the shop window, to the way the traditional cooking process is presented with stylish copper pans simmering away gently in the glass-walled kitchen.

The immaculately turned-out staff are multi-skilled and work across the shop, in the kitchen and on the brand's communications. They are recruited for their love of 1930s and 1940s culture, having got to know one another as friends first, at swing dances. Such a recruitment policy creates a warm and happy atmosphere for staff and visitors alike.

'I wanted to start my own business creating something sweet and beautiful that made people happy! We are a small company, and make almost everything we need in-house, so we can go from idea to physical product fast - whether that's a new flavour or new packaging.'
- Lisa Ericson

Address
Nytorgsgatan 38, 116 40 Stockholm, Sweden
Website
www.parlanskonfektyr.se
Founder
Lisa Ericson

The details of a shopkeeper's dress code speak silent volumes about their belief in their business and its narrative.

TIPS

· · · · · · ·

TIP 1 - The tiniest details can make a big collective impression on your customers, so consider every little touchpoint, from the style of your packaging to the music you play in the background.

· · · · · · ·

TIP 2 - The way you style your packaged products can notably increase the desire to purchase. This applies to your shop displays, of course, but also to the photographs for your website and other e-commerce.

· · · · · · ·

TIP 3 - Dress to impress. You are part of your brand story, and your personal style will have an impact on your audience as soon as they step through the door.

Charming vintage wallpapers combat the white space that is usually found in the backgrounds of product photography.

welcome

to the   #chö

chocolate   #cro

kitchen

#chöklovers   b

CHÖK
BARCELONA, SPAIN
···

With a background in international food and drinks, Fernando Madrid left the corporate world to set up Chök, 'the chocolate kitchen'. His vision was to create a participatory space where customers can not only enjoy freshly made treats, but also learn how to cook with chocolate as an ingredient in a variety of cuisines and dishes, from fish and meat to salads. His mission is to educate about and promote the use of good chocolate in the kitchen, as well as to develop a popular chain of chocolate-based bakeries.

Madrid has so far opened two locations, each of which is part shop, part kitchen and part workshop. The styles of the spaces are deliberately different, referencing the surrounding neighbourhoods and the appealing, varied decor of both modern and traditional kitchens. Just as with the food itself, great care is taken with every little detail of the presentation, communication, branding, packaging and signage.

Popular features include the wall of doughnuts, where the freshly iced rings are displayed on wooden hoopla-style poles; and the tactile, hand-stamped packaging that is offered at the wrapping table. Written communication is minimal, with a simple typewriter font used on individual letter cards. Everything in the airy, daylit spaces is created to communicate the idea of freshness, with a happy, home-made feel - but also with an edge of the innovation and experimentation that always come from the kitchen.

'When I started the business nothing like this existed. We must be profitable, so we sell many doughnuts, but we also make opportunities to share the skills that are required to cook with chocolate at home. Through our workshops we involve our customers more deeply and happily in our business.'
- Fernando Madrid

Addresses
Carrer de les Ramalleres 26 and Carrer del Carme 3,
08001 Barcelona, Spain
Website
www.chokbarcelona.com
Founder
Fernando Madrid
Designer
Montse Vicens, Intsight (www.int-sight.com)

Rubber-stamping on packaging
materials adds a delightful,
craft-led touch that enhances
the products' home-made feel.

TIPS

. . . .

TIP 1 - You don't have to display your fresh produce in the expected way. If your products have a quirky characteristic, make the most of that feature and see people smile.

. . . .

TIP 2 - Showing that you care about the details of your presentation demonstrates that you care about the details of your products and your business as a whole, too. Don't lose the personal touch.

. . . .

TIP 3 - Customers love beautiful, pleasing packaging, but you can still keep it simple. Set up a wrapping station to bring joy to the process with string, stickers and rubber stamps.

The art of packaging is celebrated as the finishing touch to the customer's experience, created through little details and a dedicated wrapping table.

chök
the chocolate
kitchen

BEER STORE VIENNA
VIENNA, AUSTRIA
...

After a first career in engineering, Johannes Grohs was looking for a new adventure and a new business in which to immerse himself. Being a lover of craft beer, he decided to set up a business and shop with the promise of scouting, discovering and introducing the best range of craft beers to receptive audiences in Vienna. The resulting retail operation, although focused on Austrian audiences, has become a highly acclaimed destination with an international customer base, and it also now runs a large annual beer festival.

Central to Grohs and his business partner Alexander Beinhauer's proposition is a dedication to providing the highest-quality, expert service that is personal and attentive. In the shop, which they claim is the only craft-beer store of its kind, there is deliberately no self-service option for customers: rather than shelves stacked with boxes and bottles, there are simply sample bottles on display.

All the beers are kept in a specially built cold-storage room, and customers can sample anything from stock while sitting in the relaxed tasting lounge area in the centre of the shop. The Beer Store claims that such a scale of tasting service is unique in the world.

The style of the shop is deliberately rustic and retro. Grohs and Beinhauer evolve and build it all themselves from reclaimed and vintage materials and furnishings, with the aim of creating a simple, relaxed living room where customers can spend time comfortably and informally learning about and appreciating great beer, before leaving with a personal selection with which they are delighted.

'People return because of the personal contact, talking to a real person who is a genuine expert and who focuses on finding the perfect product for the customer. You don't experience that if a shop is self-service. It's something for enthusiasts - and people love that.'
- Johannes Grohs

Address
Wilhelmstraße 23, 1120 Vienna, Austria
Website
www.beerstorevienna.at
Founders
Johannes Grohs and Alexander Beinhauer

TIPS

. . . .

TIP 1 – The service you offer is key to nurturing a beneficial rapport, so encourage your customers to linger for longer in a relaxed space that does not revolve around the cash desk.

. . . .

TIP 2 – If there is a lot of specialist knowledge associated with your products, consider how you can communicate that in a welcoming way that won't overwhelm the customer with facts and options.

Only one of each product is displayed, encouraging a conversation with the owner, to ensure that each customer makes an informed choice.

The shop revolves around a friendly, simple lounge area, where all customers are welcome to take a seat, join a conversation and learn about the beers on offer.

Kits for home brewing are also sold, and the potential results are demonstrated live through working set-ups and samplings.

BIG LOVE RECORDS
TOKYO, JAPAN
...

Born out of almost three decades of experience running an independent record label, working in music retail and collecting vinyl, this cosy record shop is the embodiment of the passion for discovering, producing and promoting great music that is shared by its founders, Masashi Naka and Haruka Hirata. What began as a small retail operation in a corner of the record label's office has evolved and grown into its own space, tucked away in the energetic Harajuku district of Tokyo, and has become a cultural destination for musicians and listeners alike.

The shop promotes a wide yet discerning selection of music, predominantly on vinyl only, from the founder's own Big Love Records label and other select labels, with a focus on music from outside Asia. This offering is combined with a small bar serving great craft beers; a combination that sets a welcoming, relaxed tone. Most customers are regulars, who appreciate the personal, expert offering and the community feel. Nights when a crowd gathers to watch Big Love TV, edited monthly by Naka, are particularly popular, as is the programme of intimate acoustic gigs.

The style of the shop is casual, with displays that are built and constantly evolved by the founders themselves, helped by many artist friends. Handwritten signage adds to the perception of this venture as a very personal sharing of knowledge and expertise. And, unusually by contemporary expectations, the owners do not allow customers to listen to the vinyl in the shop; instead, they focus on conversation in order to make careful and satisfying recommendations.

'The best days are when we see a new project tarted by customers who got to know each other here in the shop - recording music together, making 'zines or hosting a gig or party. That is special, and gives us renewed meaning and reminds us of our reason to exist.'
- Haruka Hirata

Address
Houei Building 3FA, 2-Chome-31-3, Jingumae,
Shibuya-ku, 150-0001 Tokyo, Japan
Website
www.bigloverecords.jp
Founders
Masashi Naka and Haruka Hirata

Record covers are visually strong and need no further explanation, so here the space has been kept simple, with the records as the focus of the shop.

TIPS

. . . .

TIP 1 - You know your product range better than anyone else, so share your knowledge and make recommendations in a way that benefits everyone. Help your customers to make happy purchases.

. . . .

TIP 2 - Offer your shop as a meeting place where fans, experts and curious passers-by can get involved, share, learn and be inspired. This can only add value to your business.

. . . .

TIP 3 - In an age of digital everything, make your space a breath of fresh air with handwritten signs and notes, artworks and contributions from passionate friends and creative contacts.

Hand-drawn signage demonstrates that care and consideration have gone into the details of what the customer sees.

TAPES Never Went Away

THE LITTLE SHOP
BRISTOL, UK
...

The artists Amber Elise and Alex Lucas opened their thriving gallery and shop in 2013 to showcase talented artists from the Bristol area. They now also attract artists from across the United Kingdom, the Netherlands and Spain.

When they first took on the lease of the shop, the exterior was painted black, but they immediately envisaged the facade as a canvas that could visually represent the promise and creativity of their business. The large-scale bunny and pineapple mural was encouraged by their landlord and has since become a much-loved local landmark, sparking many other illustrative commissions and projects.

The shop has become known for imaginative curation across regularly changing seasonal and topical themes. For each 'rotation', the two reimagine the style and eclectic decor of the space and bring in fresh new ideas, products and creative expressions. They notably pay special attention to the ceiling as a large creative canvas, paint directly on the walls to frame hanging product displays, and draw intricate details on the windows to enhance each theme.

A different artist is introduced into the shop every three months, chosen from the many applications the owners receive.

Each launch involves hosting a party to welcome the new talent and combining the in-house illustrative styles with those of the featured artist to create appealing invitations, posters and wrapping papers, expanding on the tactile, illustrative qualities of the shop effectively with care and consideration for the details.

'Word of mouth is very important to our success. Bristol has a vibrant creative community, so now most people know who we are and spread the word. And, of course, social media plays a big part, for promoting our events and featuring different artists every week.'
- Amber Elise

Address
125 Cheltenham Road, Stokes Croft,
Bristol BS6 5RR, UK
Website
www.thelittleshop.co
Founders
Amber Elise and Alex Lucas

pOp pOp PARTy
pOP At
The Little Shop
SAt 23rD ApRil
1 till 8

Every surface in the space counts: here hand-painted elements frame the products hanging on the walls, and even the ceiling has been turned into a canvas.

TIPS
· · · · · · ·

TIP 1 - *Take creative care with the details, and follow them through in every aspect of your storytelling, from the façade and windows to the posters for your in-store events.*
· · · · · · ·

TIP 2 - *If your business revolves around building a community of talent, make that visible. Your shop is a canvas for celebrating stories, so invite collaboration and benefit everyone involved.*

The bold, intricate visual style has become a trademark of the business, and is used in all its communications.

DIGITAL & CONTENT
...

YOUR WEBSITE AND ONLINE CONTENT,
LIKE YOUR SHOP WINDOW, REPRESENT
YOUR BRAND 24/7, SO INVEST
TIME IN DEVELOPING AN ENGAGING
DIGITAL STYLE.
...

'Opening a window into your own
world is a good place to begin.'
- Jeff Greenwald (b. 1954)

So far, we have explored a variety of
considerations, techniques and tools for
conceiving a compelling and effective shop
environment and experience. Each moment
of encounter, each physical and sensory
touchpoint, has a role to play individually
and as part of a collective message.

This is also the case when it comes to
a brand's online platforms and the content
that is generated to support them. In this
chapter we continue to focus on analysing
the visual techniques and approach to
content that should be considered, rather
than the business strategy of running an
online proposition. But note that these
visual encounters - as with everything
discussed in this book - should form
part of a wider strategic model for
maximum impact.

In our contemporary commercial society
- the 'digital age' - we can't deny that
online content influences almost every
consumer interaction. Even physical
encounters of customers with shopkeepers

and their propositions will in some way
have been influenced in expectation or
action by the subconscious or conscious
reach of digital information. At this point
in the twenty-first century, the potential
audience for any shop is far larger than
ever before, and considering even simple
techniques and devices associated with
an engaging online presence can bring
huge benefits.

This does not mean that every
shopkeeper must open an online shop and
invest countless hours in developing content
and nurturing an online community. It does,
however, pay to recognize and respect the
power of the internet as a channel through
which to find - and be found by - larger
audiences than would ever walk past and
discover a single physical shop.

Even if the shopkeeper's commercial
offering is delivered within the physical
premises only - with no provision for
e-commerce - it must be recognized that
more and more consumers do some research
online before taking the trouble to visit
a real shop. If they like what they see or
read online, they will probably justify
travelling further to visit; or, if they
are too far away, they will phone or email
to find out if other arrangements can be
made to purchase. The expanding options for
accessible, digitally powered collection-
and-delivery services are breaking down
this previous boundary, too, and increasing
customers' comfort with purchasing at
a distance.

A website is a window that reaches out to
the consumer world, and potential audiences;
it is active twenty-four hours a day,
across time zones and even - through visual
communication - across language barriers.
It is also a window that will draw viewers
into the shopkeeper's world and so is vital
to communicating for the greatest benefit to
the business. If this platform is executed
well, it can nurture a long-distance
audience and potential customer base, even
if it does not include an online shop.

Crafting a website represents the essence of everything that we have explored so far, but in a two-dimensional format. For that reason, it is far more complex and challenging to create an effective digital presence than the apparently simple interface suggests. The process should be respected as such, and recognition should be given to the many shopkeepers - such as those included here - who have clearly invested much time, thought and effort in developing beautiful, visually compelling online encounters.

A website offers the opportunity to explain a shop's proposition concisely yet comprehensively, in an environment that - like a physical shop - is completely controlled and curated by the shopkeeper. Even if only for a limited time, the customer's attention will be focused purely on the narrative that is being presented. The viewer has chosen to visit - you cannot 'walk past' a website - so it represents a wasted opportunity and a careless attitude

if the shopkeeper does not make the most of that encounter. The customer might wish to buy online, but if that is not offered, do not shut the door on them: inspire them with another solution.

Strategically, an online platform involves a combination of the 'four Cs' of the shopkeeper's digital checklist: communication, content, commerce and community. Each shopkeeper will choose a different balance of these four strands, but every one should consider them all in some way.

The process of defining the desired approach is in itself a good exercise in finding and summarizing a coherent narrative, a clarity of voice and purpose, for the wider proposition. All in all, then, it is a worthwhile task in which to invest time and resources.

Within the four strands, digital platforms offer a multitude of opportunities to personalize, animate and evolve the message, and to cater directly to the

emotive triggers or points of interest
of the specific audience. By contrast,
the physical shop experience, which
by nature is set to a certain, defined
landscape, may not be able to cater
so directly to this constant variety
of responses.

Where an online platform becomes
particularly interesting as a proposition
in itself, therefore, is through the
potential of the rich content. Content
can help to develop deeper narratives
for and understanding of a proposition,
and offer services and added-value
aspects that enhance, support and work
in collaboration with the physical shop.
If the two platforms can work in harmony -
rather than one feeling the imbalance and
threat of the other - truly entrepreneurial,
contemporary retail comes into its own.

OUR SHOP   WHAT'S NEW   WEDDINGS   OUR FLOWERS   OUR BOOKS   CONTACT

Established in 2006, Scarlet & Violet is a busy place full of flowers and scent, a lot of chatter, creativity and a whole load of leaves dropped on the floor.

We buy our flowers daily from the market, so each day has its different beauties and every bunch we make has its own character.

Vic Brotherson

SEE INSIDE OUR SHOP

WHAT'S NEW

WEDDINGS

OUR BOOKS

OUR FLOWERS

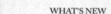

When she set up her floristry business and opened her celebrated shop in 2006, the florist Victoria Brotherson's intention was to create a space that felt more like a creative studio than a commercial venture - a place full of colour, scent, character and plenty of foliage cuttings strewn over the floor. Rather than opting for a sleek shop fit-out, she started by buying every single secondhand vase, jug, bucket and watertight container she could lay her hands on. These have now become her trademark, and her evolving collection fills the windows and adorns every surface. With this early point of differentiation, the distinctive, pretty, home-made character of the brand was born.

This delightfully nostalgic and vintage-inspired style is continued beautifully in the presentation of the brand's website. It is not a commercial platform, but acts simply as an eye-catching shop window - a celebration of the beautiful details of the Scarlet & Violet world - for the many customers who cannot visit the shop and must telephone instead.

A whimsical floral wallpaper sets the tone, against which are placed beautiful photographs of some of Brotherson's arrangements in her collection of vintage vases. Each superb image deliberately defies the usual 'white box' approach to product photography, and is styled to feel more like a tactile, rich seventeenth-century Dutch still-life painting than a contemporary commercial image of a bouquet. This website is not merely about selling flowers: it is about capturing an exquisite, dream-like vision of the joy and precious quality of floral design.

'It's crucial that the website has an element of warmth and informality. It must show what we do but also not dictate, since we tailor-make each order and the flowers change every day. I like the images to be saturated and allow the flowers to show off.'
- Victoria Brotherson

Website
www.scarletandviolet.com
Instagram
scarletandviolet
Designer
Victoria Brotherson

The stylish photography recalls seventeenth-century Dutch still lifes with its black backgrounds and intricate detail.

HELLA COCKTAIL CO.
LONG ISLAND CITY, USA
...

Beginning as a weekend project to create a great bitter for party cocktails, Hella Cocktail Co. is an acclaimed producer of handmade, small-batch cocktail ingredients including non-alcoholic mixers, syrups and bitters, stocked, served and sold widely in bars and through shops in the USA.

When they set out to create the website for their thriving business, the founders - Eddie Simeon, Tobin Ludwig and Jomaree Pinkard, also known as the 'bitter boys' - wanted to ensure a striking, photography-driven experience that would grow with and effectively represent the brand's ever-increasing portfolio of products and recipes. But, just as importantly, they needed the site to reflect the fundamental goals of their audience. It is the only destination that explains and presents the complete range of products and how to use them, so customers come to the site to purchase, to learn and to be inspired. The platform is therefore organized to offer both a streamlined shopping experience and a wealth of narrative information about the product lines, the expertise within the brand and - not least - a range of recipes and 'how to' guides to inspire engagement and purchase.

Hella Cocktail Co. is focused on empowering cocktail lovers and foodies with the tools they need to make craft cocktails in their own homes, so the imagery that is used on the site and on social media is designed to support the idea of universality. The signature creative direction is overhead shots, showing ingredients laid out in a clear, stylish, diagrammatic style. These are combined with more traditional product shots and a range of fresh, detailed close-ups of ingredients, reminding the audience of the handmade, small-batch, authentic nature of the business.

'We believe that it is critical for our content to be visually compelling. If you have only a split second to make an impression online, impactful visuals are a priority. But we also have an enthusiastic, captive audience, so sometimes it makes sense to offer more narrative-driven content, too.'
- Jomaree Pinkard

Address
23-23 Borden Avenue,
Long Island City, NY 11101, USA
Website
www.hellacocktail.co
Instagram
hellacocktailco
Founders
Jomaree Pinkard, Tobin Ludwig and Eddie Simeon

The stylish, food magazine-style product and recipe photography makes the ingredients, flavours and textures almost tactile.

Showing objects and ingredients scattered around the box helps to create a sensory image in the mind of the customer.

Coffee Spice Rubbed Spareribs

Pin it

TBAD @TheBarAtDaniels

We're all gonna' need drinks this week. I suggest a Whiskey Sour tonight #cocktails #bourbon @4RosesBourbon @HellaCompany @LUXARDOUSA

TBAD's Whiskey Sour Recipe (Makes 2 because it's good to share!)

5 ounces Bourbon (Some people like less. They're wrong.)
2 ounces lemon juice (fresh squeezed only!)
1.5 ounces simple syrup (1 cup sugar dissolved in 1 cup boiling water)
Optional: add 2-4 dashes of Ginger Lemon Bitters from Hella
1 white from a large egg (extra large is okay, NO JUMBOs)
2 Luxardo maraschino cherries for garnish
(No, you cannot use cheap cherries from the super market ice cream aisle!)

Fill the larger half of a boston shaker with ice.

Add all ingredients (except cherries) to the smaller half.

Pour ingredients over the ice, seal and shake vigorously for 30 seconds

Strain into chilled glasses. (I like a coup for this, but there is no wrong choice.)

Using a fresh peel for each drink, express oils from a lemon peel over the drink and rim the glass with the cut edge of the peel.

Garnish drink with fresh lemon peel and maraschino cherry.

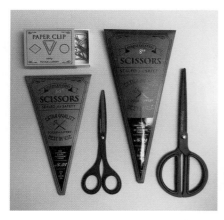

GRANDPA
STOCKHOLM, SWEDEN
...

This brand of beautifully presented lifestyle shops in Stockholm, with the affectionate name Grandpa, was founded by Jonas Pelz, Anders Johansson and Martin Sundberg with the aim of creating a place in the city both for shopping and for just 'hanging out'. Devised before the now widespread idea of the 'concept store' existed on the high street, the brand has continued to evolve in directions that allow it to retain its individuality in the marketplace. One notably strong asset that sets it apart is the way the team approaches its digital offering.

With an ethos that echoes that of the shops, the website offers a fine selection of lifestyle products for purchase. These products are also compellingly promoted in snapshots and still-life imagery on Instagram, an increasingly effective platform for the brand in reaching its now international audience.

But beyond commerce, as a method of encouraging visitors to linger for longer and to feel more engaged with the brand and its network of talent, the website is also a platform for screening a unique content proposition: Grandpa TV. This idea was launched in 2010, before social channels could really give it enough leverage, but the 'creative chat show' concept - filmed on a sofa in the brand's beautifully curated flagship store - has since found greater traction, and has proved to be an appealing method of brand differentiation. In fact, it has been so well received that it has now developed into a sister business, Grandpa Electric, producing high-quality cultural material and short films for the retailer's commercial partners, among other clients.

'At first we just thought that Grandpa TV would be a fun thing to do. We have nurtured a great network, and the idea of a chat show with interesting people appealed to us. Artists, actors, designers, musicians, stylists, club organizers - everyone featured is connected to Grandpa, as a customer or through creating something with us.'
- Jonas Pelz

Website
www.grandpa.se
Instagram
grandpastore
Founders
Jonas Pelz, Anders Johansson and Martin Sundberg
Content
Grandpa Electric (www.grandpaelectric.se)

Episodes of the Grandpa web series are filmed in the shop, with customers featuring as part of the background scene.

The Grandpa show - Episod 15 - Ida Redig & Fredrik Wikholm

THE GRANDPA SHOW

4:51 / 20:05

Precision of layout gives a compelling, polished feel to the product photography for the e-commerce platform.

The Grandpa show - Episod 20 - Salvatore Scappini & Ch...

The Grandpa show - Episod 19 - Elsa Billgren & Titiyo

The Grandpa show - Episod 18 - Vanessa Falk & Martin "...

The Grandpa Show - Episod 17 - Isabelle McAllister & Eri...

SHANE CONFECTIONERY
PHILADELPHIA, USA
...

After operating for ninety-nine years under the ownership of the Shane family, this traditional confectionery business was bequeathed in 2010 to local brothers Ryan and Eric Berley, who had built up a reputation for nurturing high-quality, nostalgic sweet offerings through their nearby old-time ice-cream saloon, The Franklin Fountain. After taking eighteen months to restore the sweetshop to its nineteenth-century glory, the brothers decided to keep the original brand name in order to commemorate the great confectionery-making family, and to preserve a strong Philadelphia tradition.

As well as working hard to maintain the quality and character of the celebrated business and the products it makes in-house, the brothers wanted to be able to serve a new audience, one that would come from ever further afield via the internet. They developed a website and e-commerce platform serving customers in the United States and Europe, but put the standard rules of traditional website design to one side. Reflecting the turn-of-the-century style of the shop, they chose instead to build a site that feels almost tactile, more analogue scrapbook than digital wireframe, with a multitude of thoughtful, eclectic details.

The imagery is a combination of original celluloids, diagrams and sketches of products - many of which have changed little in more than a century - and new product photography for the online shop, shot in a style that gives it the same nostalgic slant. It is presented within a digitized version of a leather-bound ledger, complete with real, photographed details such as photo corners and ribbons. Completing the illusion, the book appears to be placed on a background of white marble - the traditional slab on which candy mixtures are prepared.

'We wanted our website to have a turn-of-the-century feel. In the late 1800s and early 1900s businesses often kept scrapbooks for memorabilia. Our website is a modern interpretation of that. We believe in quality and authenticity in every aspect of our business, and our website is no exception.'
- Ryan Berley

Address
110 Market Street, Philadelphia, PA 19106, USA
Website
www.shanecandies.com
Instagram
shaneconfectionery
Founders
Eric and Ryan Berley

Seek:

Order Candy Here

Established 1911

Est. 1911

SHANE CANDIES
110 MARKET STREET
PHILADELPHIA, PA. 19106

of thanks begin in the heart
hey begin as a kernel of light

sgiving Day

Shop Hovrs
Sunday through Thursday
11am to 8 o'clock pm
Friday & Saturday
11am to 11 o'clock pm

HISTORY AND REBIRTH

SHOP NOW!

CANDY-MAKING

PRIVATE EVENTS

SEASONAL

OG

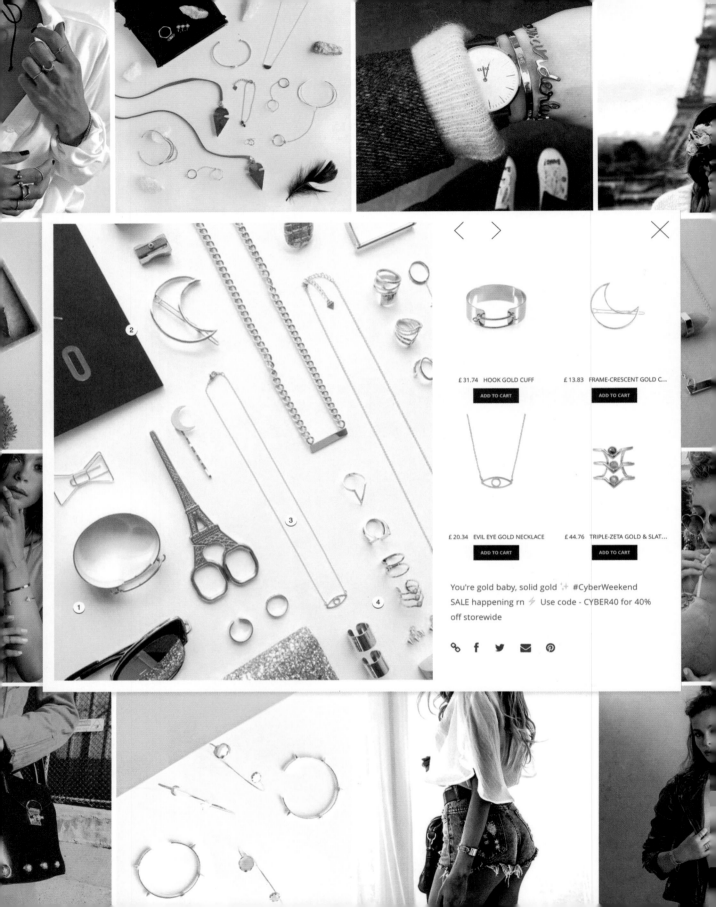

£ 31.74   HOOK GOLD CUFF

ADD TO CART

£ 13.83   FRAME-CRESCENT GOLD C...

ADD TO CART

£ 20.34   EVIL EYE GOLD NECKLACE

ADD TO CART

£ 44.76   TRIPLE-ZETA GOLD & SLAT...

ADD TO CART

You're gold baby, solid gold ✨ #CyberWeekend SALE happening rn ⚡ Use code - CYBER40 for 40% off storewide

WANDERLUST + CO.
KUALA LUMPUR, MALAYSIA
...

Founded by the entrepreneur Jennifer Low in Melbourne, Australia, this energetic and empowered jewellery label has since moved with her to her new home and studio in Malaysia, and still exudes the warmth of personality and attention to detail that it did when she began it in 2010. The label is loved by the international A-list crowd, but prides itself on offering a collection for all girls - with a belief that 'she is whoever she wants to be' - giving its audience the freedom to experiment, style and get creative at an affordable price, and ultimately to 'choose extraordinary over ordinary'.

The brand has an ever-growing online retail presence, and more than 400 wholesale stockists globally, but does not have its own shops. Instead, the carefully merchandized website acts as the global flagship store, with a strong focus on community-building through stylish, engaging visual content. This material is placed strategically on social media channels - most notably Instagram - and, through the addition of a smart, interactive layer over the images, customers can click on any piece that catches their eye to connect directly to the online shop and purchase it.

The goal of all the visual content is to maintain an aspirational message that encourages the positive spirit associated with the label. The evolving image collection is carefully thought through to be consistent, on-trend and relevant. Style images and tips tend to be most popular, but the selection also includes ad hoc images of celebrities and influencers seen wearing key pieces, and more creative inspirational snapshots, giving the overall feel of an online magazine rather than a commercial operation.

'We love being part of open conversations with our customers. Seeing our pieces being part of milestones and moments in their daily adventures has been, and will always be, what drives us to keep doing what we do.'
- Jennifer Low

Website
www.wanderlustandco.com
Instagram
wanderlustandco
Founder
Jennifer Low

HIUT DENIM CO.
CARDIGAN, WALES
...

For three decades, the small town of Cardigan in west Wales was home to a thriving community of workers making jeans for brands across the fashion industry. At its peak it produced 35,000 pairs a week. Then the competitive industry moved overseas and the factories closed. But the entrepreneurs David and Clare Hieatt recognized that a wealth of skill was still present in the town, so they founded the Hiut Denim Co. with the aim of reigniting and nurturing local manufacturing.

The small, celebrated company is dedicated to building an authentic brand that is focused on the production process, and not on scaling to a commercial structure that requires its own shops. However, its audience reach is wide and demand for the limited-edition denim products substantial, through the awareness the team has nurtured via a savvy and refined digital communications strategy and associated events and collaborative pop-ups.

The website is the predominant platform for representing the brand and telling its stories, supported by well-curated social, community-building assets including email newsletters rich in cultural content that reaches far and wide to illustrate the inspiration of the business. In contrast to all the digital activity, they also release limited-edition, highly covetable printed output.

The company's motto is 'Do One Thing Well'. Although that ethos is applied predominantly to its dedicated manufacturing process, it also holds true for the careful and focused way in which the team is building a wider content-led narrative that complements the products.

'Quality is what we make. It's what we stand for. It's what we believe in. But it's not how we will sell our jeans. People have desires and dreams, and you have to learn how to make your product fit into them. People buy a lifestyle, an image, a purpose.'
- David Hieatt

Website
www.hiutdenim.co.uk
Instagram
hiutdenim
Founders
David and Clare Hieatt

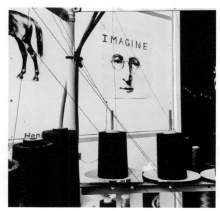

Ingenious ways of weaving content into the brand experience include Spotify playlists streamed via a bespoke digital radio.

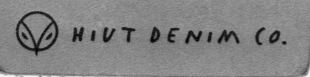

The brand's well-curated email newsletters look almost like tangible, tactile scrapbooks full of treasured artefacts.

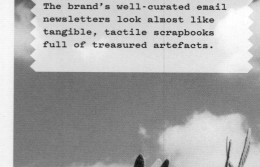

Do One Thing Well
November 29th 2016
The 'Scrapbook Chronicles' will bookmark what caught our eye, the stuff that inspired us, and log what we are up to as a small denim company making our way in this world. I hope you enjoy them.

Zimbabwe Cotton Short Run.
In order to make a great selvedge, go and find the best cotton in the world. That's what Nihon Menpu did for our latest short run. Last few left. Once they're gone. They're gone.

The Best Air-Cleaning Plants for Your Home.
According to NASA.

The images and content created
to tell the brand story are
irreverent and authentic, with
an aspirational, joyful quality.

PHOTO CREDITS

...

2: Shelving from the Gekaapt pop-up shop in Amsterdam (page 146).4: A wall display by the New Craftsmen for Makers House in London (page 202). 12r: Appear Here (www.appearhere.co.uk); 13: Robert Adalierd; 19: Appear Here (www.appearhere.co.uk); 25-27: Robert Adalierd; 33: Fabian Öhrn; 36r: Pedro Sadio; 43-45: Paul Grundy; 56-59: Pedro Sadio; 66l: Mira Schroeder; 66r: Walt Agency; 67l: Sophie de Lignerolles; 67r: Natalia Apezetxea; 68-73: Alastair Hendy; 75 and 76t: Walt Agency; 76b and 77br: Lionel Moreau; 77t and bl: © Le Comptoir Général; 78-81: Sophie de Lignerolles; 83, 84tl, 85tl: Tim Schroeder; 84tr and b: Ludgar Paffrath; 85tr and b: Mustafah Abdulaziz; 89t: A-2-O Studio; 91-93: Natalia Apezetxea; 96r: Julie Koch; 102-5: Joel Bukiewicz; 118-21: Julie Koch; 125l: Cathelijne van der Lande; 127-29: Miyuki Kaneko; 135: Sonja Velda; 136tl and b: Sarah Distel; 136tr and 137: Cathelijne van der Lande; 142-45: Tuulia Kolehmainen; 152l: Achin Hatzius; 152r: Kara Rosenlund; 153: Jolanda Kruse; 155-57: Kara Rosenlund; 158-61: Karl Donovan; 163-65: Filip Šach; 166-69: Jolanda Kruse; 171-73: Achim Hatzius; 174-77: Studio Dubuisson; 180l: Steve Herud; 186-89: Konrad Ćwik; 199-201: Steve Herud; 210l: Ross Fraser McLean/StudioRoRo; 210r: Lit Ma; 211r: Panagiotis Voumvakis; 212-17: Joachim Gern; 219-21: Lit Ma; 227: Panagiotis Voumvakis; 228, 230-31, 232b, 233b: Ross Fraser McLean/StudioRoRo; 232tl, tr, 233t: Future Positive Studio; 235: Óskar Þórðarson; 238l and 245-47: Joline Fransson; 286t: weareknit.co.uk

All back cover images taken from inside the book.

First published in the United Kingdom in 2017 by Thames & Hudson Ltd, 181A High Holborn, London WC1V 7QX

The Creative Shopkeeper © 2017 Lucy Johnston

Designed by Supple Studio

British Library Cataloguing-in-Publication Data
A catalogue record for this book is available from the British Library

ISBN 978-0-500-51961-5

Printed and bound by C&C Offset Printing Co. Ltd, China

To find out about all our publications, please visit **www.thamesandhudson.com**. There you can subscribe to our e-newsletter, browse or download our current catalogue, and buy any titles that are in print.